Emyl Jenkins'

Reproduction

Furniture

Emyl Jenkins'
Reproduction
Furniture

ANTIQUES FOR

THE NEXT GENERATION

Crown Publishers, Inc. New York

For Nancy Evans

and

Buck and Lucy Menius

Good friends

who love good furniture,

regardless of its age

In memory of

N. I. Beinenstock

For all of his contributions as

a gentleman and scholar,

but especially for the founding of

The Furniture Library,

High Point, North Carolina

Published by Crown Publishers, Inc., 201 East 50th Street, New York, New York 10022. Member of the Crown Publishing Group.

Random House, Inc. New York, Toronto, London, Sydney, Auckland

CROWN is a trademark of Crown Publishers, Inc.

Manufactured in the United States of America

Design by Lauren Dong

Library of Congress Cataloging-in-Publication Data
Jenkins, Emyl.
    Emyl Jenkins' reproduction furniture: antiques for the next generation / Emyl Jenkins.
        p.   cm.
    Includes bibliographical references and index.
    1. Furniture industry and trade—History—19th century.
2. Furniture industry and trade—History—20th century. 3. Furniture—Reproduction—Collectors and collecting. 4. Furniture—Antiques.
5. Furniture—Expertizing. 6. Furniture—United States—History—19th century. 7. Furniture—United States—History—20th century. I. Title. II. Title: Reproduction furniture
III. Title: Antiques for the next generation.
TS880.J46   1995
684.104'0973—dc20   94-41393
                    CIP

ISBN 0-517-58527-8
10 9 8 7 6 5 4 3 2 1
First Edition

Contents

Foreword

by Ralph and Terry Kovel

It's easy to look up a furniture maker who worked in America before 1900. It's even possible to learn about the innovators behind the Arts and Crafts, Art Deco, and Fifties furniture. But until now it has been almost impossible to identify the pieces of furniture that Grandma might have bought at a local store in 1930. *Emyl Jenkins' Reproduction Furniture* is the first book to take an in-depth look at this furniture made for American homes during the first part of the century.

Collectors and historians are just now starting to reassess the artistic value and important place of mainstream twentieth-century American furniture. Much of this furniture is well built, made of solid wood, and may even have some type of hand carving or hand-rubbed finish. Many authentic reproductions were so accurately made that today sometimes they could pass for acutal eighteenth-century pieces

During the Kennedy years, when the White House was being restored, many rare antiques were donated, including a piece of Baltimore furniture with eglomise decoration. Several years went by before this piece was identified as a later copy, not an early-nineteenth-century prize. Emyl Jenkins' book shows hundreds of reproduction pieces that could be confused with antiques. Pieces ranging from William and Mary to 1940s modern are pictured here.

And the sometimes strange hybrid styles that are really twentieth-century revivals of several different early designs are studied with an unprejudiced eye. It is difficult to look at those type of pieces from Grandma's house without thinking they are old-fashioned and perhaps in poor taste, but Emyl explains which styles are good and which styles are bad, and makes it clear why Grandma decorated the way she did.

One of the most valuable chapters for collectors is the directory, a list of companies and their furniture products, which gives information about where and when they worked. And as an added feature, a bibliography of books and catalogs, old and new, will help those who want to learn more. Uncovering the history of a maker and the origins of a design may not be enough, so Emyl includes pricing guidelines for the most commonly found pieces of reproduction furniture.

Emyl Jenkins is well known as an appraiser, researcher, author, and historian. Her talents make this, the first serious look at twentieth-century American reproduction furniture, a book that will remain a standard. Already a surge of interest in early-twentieth-century reproduction pieces has sparked a rise in prices at resale and antiques shops and auctions. Trust Emyl to write this easy-to-read reference book for collectors at all levels.

Too little is known about the fine-quality reproduction furniture that our ancestors bought with pride. They had every right to be proud of their new purchases, for furniture like this Berkey and Gay bedroom suite, copied after furniture designs attributed to the great 18th-century New England craftsman John Goddard, is holding up well today in both style and durability.

As proof that Goddard's work, and the demand for copies of his pieces, has stood the test of time, here is a 1990s American copy of an 18th-century classic, the Sutton reproduction of a Goddard shell-carved kneehole desk. (Photo courtesy of Sutton Collection/Century Furniture Industries)

Introduction

American-Made Reproduction Furniture: Too Good to Toss Out

Reproduction furniture. Few phrases could sound more dull, less exciting, or more unglamorous.

Tell someone "I've got some old reproduction furniture" and the listener immediately pictures nondescript mass-produced copies of beautiful, deeply patinated antiques. The implied connotation is that a piece of reproduction furniture is something you have when you can't afford the real thing—or worse yet, when you can't distinguish the real thing from the reproduction.

Add to those negatives the casual statement I, as an appraiser, so often hear, "Don't waste your time looking at that old piece. It's just an old reproduction," and the unspoken implication is that older reproduction furniture isn't worth a second glance, and it certainly has no

real monetary value. In short, it is no more than "used goods."

This is unfortunate, because many honest, well-constructed, and artfully crafted "old reproductions" are of finer quality and worth more money than the glut of overpriced, fake, made-up, altered, or generally inferior pieces that are being sold as "antiques" these days. Many old reproductions are literally too good to toss out.

The problem is that few people know much about their grandparents' or great-grandparents' store-bought furniture. Most have only heard a few sentimental family stories about Papa's chair or Aunt Mary's dressing table. If you really want to be able to tell how old and how fine a piece of furniture is, you need to know the history of how these pieces came to be.

It was about 11:00 A.M. on a picture-perfect early June Sunday. I was on a pleasure-only trip in the Far West. "No work today," I had promised myself and my friend. But when we stopped for gas and I saw the lady opening the door to the antiques shop, I quickly ducked in behind her. "Just looking," I called over my shoulder. Within thirty seconds I was dashing back to the car to grab my camera. "When will people learn?" I asked, and my friend and I both knew my promise was broken.

You see, I've always thought that if I know something, then everyone else knows it, too. Just inside the door of the shop, as big as day, was a turn-of-the-century American-made reproduction of a vargueño, a type of early Spanish desk. These pieces had been immensely popular during the years 1910–19, and I was curious to see how it was priced. There, spread out on the writing slant, in addition to the $5,995 price tag, was the picture of a period vargueño featured on page 308 of a recent Miller's Price Guide. That one dated from the 17th century and had sold at

Christie's for $17,161. Accompanying was a notation that the interior compartments (all the little drawers) of the vargueño that I could purchase for only $5,995 "may be late 18th or early 19th century," with the implication being, of course, that the case dated from the 17th century. I snapped a couple of shots (opposite) and ducked out. You see, it isn't my intention to accuse someone of false claims or advertising. Rather, it is my wish for more people, especially those in the trade, to become more knowledgeable about what they are looking at.

There really was little about the 20th-century American-made reproduction vargueño that would resemble a period 17th-century one other than its basic form. Everything about the later-made vargueño screamed "20th-century adaptation," from the type of wood and decorative motifs, to the use of modern screws and hinges, to its condition. The shop owner who was selling the piece most likely had never seen a period vargueño—there aren't that many of them around, and certainly not in the United States. But she surely has had the chance to see

these pieces and appreciate them for what they are. Hey, that vargueño is a great-looking piece in the right setting. It shouldn't be damned by a smart aleck who says, "But it's not a period piece." It should be enjoyed and appreciated by someone who says, "Isn't it a great reproduction!"

plenty of American-made reproduction furniture, because they make up the bulk of furnishings found in most homes today. The problem was she probably never thought that an American furniture company would make anything that looked like this.

Well, they did. Here (left) is an illustration from the Kittinger 1928 catalog of one so similar to the piece offered for sale that it could be its first cousin. That is the purpose of this book. I have written it to open everyone's eyes to what the American furniture manufacturers were making, and when, so we can recognize

Its Time Has Come

Over the past hundred years, the approximate time during which reproduction furniture has been made, countless books and articles have been written about *antique* furniture. Most of these concentrate on the different styles and their history. Many others, including my own *Guide to Buying and Collecting Early American Furniture,* painstakingly instruct the would-be antiques collector on how to distinguish true eighteenth- or early-nineteenth-century antiques (those pieces called "period pieces" that were made during the original time frame when the design originated) from later-made reproductions that imitate the early pieces.

Little has been written about reproduction furniture made in America during the late nineteenth and early twentieth centuries. This lack of information fuels the quickly drawn conclusion that these reproduction pieces must not be very well made.

Yet American reproduction furniture made before the 1950s—copies of the Jacobean, Queen Anne, Chippendale, Hepplewhite, Sheraton, and even Empire and Victorian pieces, plus French, Spanish, and Italian pieces—make up a major portion of the furniture found in American homes in the 1990s. The time has come to learn about the rich heritage that brought this furniture first into our ancestors' homes, and now into our own homes.

A Fresh Look at "Old Stuff"

In the past, the lack of interest in reproduction furniture could be summed up in four words: It isn't old enough. But as we rapidly approach the twenty-first century, many of these pieces are

Pieces like this 17th-century–style bench and court cupboard are often mislabeled "English, 19th-century" in antiques shops and auctions. They have such a warm color and are so well copied after the period pieces that it is assumed they were made in England. In reality, these and many other distinctly English and European pieces were made by American furniture companies during the early 20th century. These two pieces were made by Kittinger in the late 1920s.

actually reaching the "magical" one-hundred-year-old mark.

Suddenly this "old stuff," as it is often referred to, is qualifying for the legal definition of an antique—an item that is one hundred years old or older. As my friend Kay Miller once said, "Maybe we ought to stop and think that if we say that something is 'just old stuff,' today it's probably old enough to have some value!"

After all, today's young people in the midst of furnishing their first homes are now genuinely interested in the furniture made during the first half of this century. And so they should be, for as a favorite saying of mine goes, "Your parents have atrocious taste. Your grandparents had acceptable taste. But your great-grandparents had superlative taste!"

It was today's younger generation's grandparents and great-grandparents who bought reproduction furniture to furnish their own "first homes" sixty, seventy-five, or ninety years ago. These young folks now think Granny's old furniture is grand.

Just listen to what they say about it.

"Look at the solid wood." "The old finish is so mellow." "You couldn't buy a new piece like that today." "See how well it is constructed. Those are real dovetails and that's real poplar inside the drawers!"

In short, they like the *look* and the *feel* of the very same furniture that many older people casually toss off as "secondhand furniture."

Not long ago, a nineteen-year-old college student seated by me on an airplane told me in the most loving and glowing terms how she treasures the bedroom suite that her ninety-year-old grandmother recently told her she planned to leave to her. It has twin beds, a vanity with three-sectional mirror and stool, a bedside table, side chair, and a chest of drawers, she said. "I've seen some pieces just like mine in shops and at sales, but I've never seen the *whole suite* all together," she exclaimed starry eyed. (You can be sure that when this young lady has her own home she will want to furnish it with other pieces from the same 1920s era as her prized bedroom suite.)

Add to these comments the fact that the supply of eighteenth- and early-nineteenth-century period antiques continues to dwindle while the demand continues to increase (as do the prices), and you quickly realize there's a practical reason

Not everyone could afford or even wanted faithful copies of period pieces. Suites of furniture adapted to "modern" life and homes and loosely based on classical furniture styles were gobbled up by newlyweds to fill their homes on every street in every town in the United States during the years 1910–19 and the 1920s. This mahogany-veneered, three-sectional mirrored dressing table topped with a fanciful Adam-style urn and swag motif is typical of the medium-priced furniture so immensely popular at the time.

why there is new interest in the old copies that date from fifty, seventy, and a hundred years ago.

Many of these pieces are of excellent quality and design. They supply the "look" of the period pieces, and most important, they are still affordable. That's a winning combination.

The Changing Perception

Some people are no doubt surprised that I have chosen to write a book on American-made reproduction furniture. But my aim is to inform and educate people about these often undervalued and unappreciated pieces.

Over the years I have watched the prices of the mass-manufactured reproduction pieces steadily creep upward. I have seen people later regret that they sold their ancestors' reproduction pieces. And I have heard people bemoan the fact that they didn't buy more of this furniture when the pieces were still "steals." A few years from now we will all look back and wistfully remark, "I wish I could buy that furniture now for what it cost back in the mid-1990s."

Here, then, is my guide to help you understand exactly what you are buying when you purchase an old reproduction, whether it be a Chippendale-style chair, a Louis XVI–style commode, an Empire-style sofa, a Hepplewhite-style Pembroke table, or an entire suite of bedroom furniture loosely based on the Queen Anne style.

Or, if you are one of the lucky ones inheriting an ancestor's furniture and you must make selec-

The trained eye immediately knows that this set of chairs could never have been made during Queen Anne's reign. For starters, the legs are too spindly, the frame around the back is too far distanced from the center splat, and the feet are all wrong for the 18th century. These are reproduction chairs that have the general characteristics of period Queen Anne chairs—cabriole legs, vase-shaped backsplat, and shell carving. However a century or so later, each one of these characteristics is changed ever so slightly and the chairs have a distinct "reproduction" look to them. (Photo by David Nicolay, courtesy of Neal Auction Company)

It is difficult to tell whether a piece might be a period antique or not when the original form is faithfully executed and the piece was made to look "old" when it was made some eighty or more years ago. Experts get fooled every day. It takes a vast knowledge of tools and materials to make the distinction between the truly antique and the piece that, as the dealers say, "has a lot of age to it." But once you become aware of the number of "authentic reproductions" like those made by such companies as John Miller (above), you will become one of the relatively small percentage of antiques lovers who are readily attuned to just *how* many *reproductions were actually made in America at the turn of the century.*

tions from among the items, this book will help you determine how to make your choices—what to keep and what to discard or pass on to others.

Distinguishing Quality

There have always been both good- and bad-quality reproduction pieces. Some are painstakingly handcrafted, beautifully designed, and precisely measured copies that can be difficult to distinguish from true period pieces.

Others are fanciful, and sometimes poorly designed, adaptations of several different eighteenth- and nineteenth-century styles made from

inferior materials. Yet over the years, I have found that a large portion of the furniture-buying public does not know how to make such distinctions. They simply lump all "old reproduction" furniture together under one generic heading.

I have always felt that learning something about the construction techniques used, understanding why reproduction furniture became so popular in the first place, and knowing how to

The connoisseur would not give this "vintage" rocker a second glance. The form was never made in the 18th century, and even when it was made in the early 20th century no one seems to have given much thought to how to make it graceful or pretty. Furthermore, it was made of second-rate materials. Thousands of these rockers were made by American reproduction furniture companies and sold for $10, $15, or $20. Unfortunately, many people think this is typical of the best the companies made. Nothing could be further from the truth.

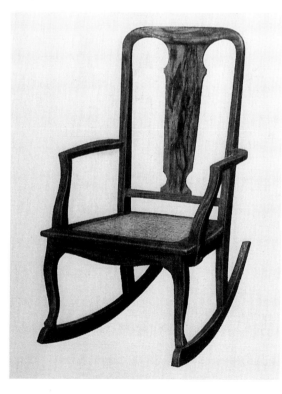

identify the various styles and determine the quality of different pieces would lead to a greater appreciation of this overlooked era of American-made reproduction furniture.

To that end I have written this book. But looking at the scope of material that *could* have been included in these pages, I feel like the eighteenth-century writers who began their books with "apologies." "Dear Reader," these tomes began, followed by reasons why the writer was inadequate to treat his subject matter as fully or as richly as he wished.

The Author's Apology

"Dear Reader," I long to say, "it would be impossible to list all the manufacturers of reproduction furniture in existence in the late nineteenth and early twentieth centuries, or to picture each of the countless variations of tables, chairs, chests, desks, beds, cupboards, and so on, that were created during this era. But you see, the 1926 *Furniture Dealers' Reference Book* alone is 598 pages long! Were I to put everything in this book that I want to, you couldn't pick it up."

To those who think antiques are the only fine furnishings suitable for grand houses, I gently suggest a visit to some of the truly great houses that were furnished in a mixture of antiques and reproductions in the years 1910–19, 1920s, and 1930s. This view of the living room of Reynolda House comes from one such home. It was built in 1917 by R. J. Reynolds in Winston-Salem, North Carolina, and remains a prime example of the taste for quality furnishings in that era.

Indeed, trade catalogs and old magazines are the richest source for information on reproduction furniture made in the United States at the turn of the century and into the first half of the twentieth century. They are filled with wonderful illustrations and articles about the furniture styles and designs, trends in interior design, architecture, manufacturing techniques, furniture lines and companies, and the industrial changes of the time. They provide the best primary material for information about the furniture of this era. Yet who has access to these materials, or the time to read and digest it all? You have to pick and choose.

That is what I have had to do. In these pages you will find information about the best-known companies and most popular styles—pieces like those I have seen over the years in my clients' and friends' homes.

> Now and then a person born under a lucky star is able to buy antiques which match his own old pieces, but such fortune is so rare, considering the number of seekers for the old, that we leave it out of the question. Modern pieces that shall match the old in type and character are the only alternative. But fake "antiquing" has so prejudiced the minds of the honest portion of the public that they cry out against all reproductions from the antique.
>
> —ART AND DECORATION, DECEMBER 1915

For readers or students who wish more technical information and a deeper sociological explanation on this fascinating subject than I can offer in these pages, I recommend two books.

Chicago Furniture: Art, Craft, & Industry, 1833–1983, by Sharon Darling, written in 1984, deals specifically and in great detail with the manufacturing of the furniture. Though the main emphasis of Darling's well-paced and easy-to-read survey is Chicago's furniture industry, the other manufacturing centers—Jamestown, New York; Grand Rapids, Michigan; and Thomasville, North Carolina—mirrored the evolution and development that occurred in Chicago.

The Tastemakers by Russell Lynes is a fascinating and brilliantly written history of our American culture. Though published in 1949, it explains better than any more recent book why the mainstream of our late-nineteenth- and early-twentieth-century ancestors preferred reproductions of earlier styles over newer, more "modern" styles.

Yet because I could find no single illustrated book that showed how the popular mind-set of the day *and* the technical evolution came together at just the right time in history to create the demand for reproduction furniture in America, I undertook the task.

Just as the furniture of this period was for the people, so this book is for the people. It could be much more scholarly, but scholars can and will dig deeper. My hope is that the information pro-

Who, What, Where, When, How, and Why

But there is more than just knowing *who* made such and such a piece and *what* style it is. Like the tried and true journalism jingle, "who, what, where, when, how, and why," an understanding of *how* and *where* the furniture was made, plus *when* and *why* these styles came to be so popular—in other words the technology and sociology behind reproduction furniture—adds to our appreciation of the objects themselves.

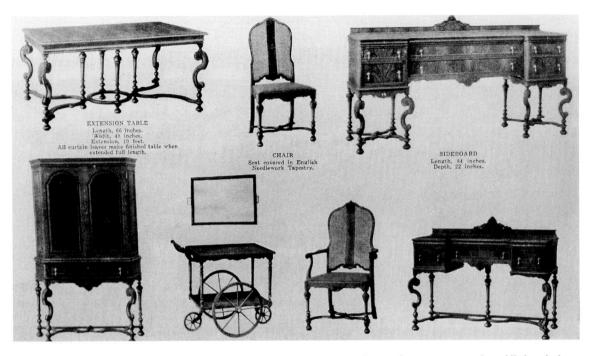

Without question, the best source for information on American-made reproduction furniture is an archive filled with the old magazines, newspaper ads, and furniture catalogs of the period. Here you see everything from the purest, line-measured faithful copy to fanciful Queen Anne–style tea carts and Chippendale twin bed suites. These two pages from Good Furniture *magazine (above and opposite) show one company's line of Jacobean-style reproductions as it would be advertised in a catalog and as the same group would be tastefully arranged in a scrumptuous room. No wonder it was so appealing to our ancestors.*

vided by the text and the pictures will be a starting point, not an end, to a new appreciation of this overlooked period of American reproduction furniture.

Using this Book

Reproduction Furniture: Antiques for the Next Generation is written to help you understand and appreciate mass-manufactured reproduction-style furniture.

Chapters 1 through 5 touch upon the combined technological, historical, and sociological events that influenced the direction of the American furniture industry as they related to reproduction furniture.

Chapters 6 and 7 deal with the furniture styles. Descriptions of the various classical styles that comprise reproduction furniture made in America will help you to quickly identify such pieces when you see them. Also included are "new" forms that were based on old styles; in other words, pieces in traditional styles that were made to accommodate the changing lifestyles of the late nineteenth and early twentieth centuries—for example, a Chippendale-style bar or Sheraton-style coffee table.

These chapters will also help you learn how to assess the quality of a piece so you can better

identify potential investment pieces. Remember, telltale materials and construction often distinguish an *excellent* American reproduction furniture piece from one that is similar in outward appearance but of lesser value.

In the directory are the names of many of the companies that produced the millions of pieces of reproduction furniture made between the 1880s and 1930s which today still occupy a special place in our homes as well as our hearts, and that, in seemingly no time at all, will become the antiques of tomorrow.

Ultimately one of the real joys of knowing about and collecting American-made reproduction furniture lies in being able to find good pieces in the marketplace, in many instances knowing who the maker was, and being able to purchase them at an affordable price. Number 918 in Wallace Nutting's 1937 furniture catalog is a mahogany block-front chest of drawers. In 1937 the price was $130. When Skinner's Auction House sold one such chest in April 1989 it went for $2,200.

With this book in hand, you will better understand your family's old, but probably not-yet antique, furniture: what style it is, who made it, why they bought it, how good it really is, and even what it may be worth.

PART ONE

Furniture for the People: 1850–1890

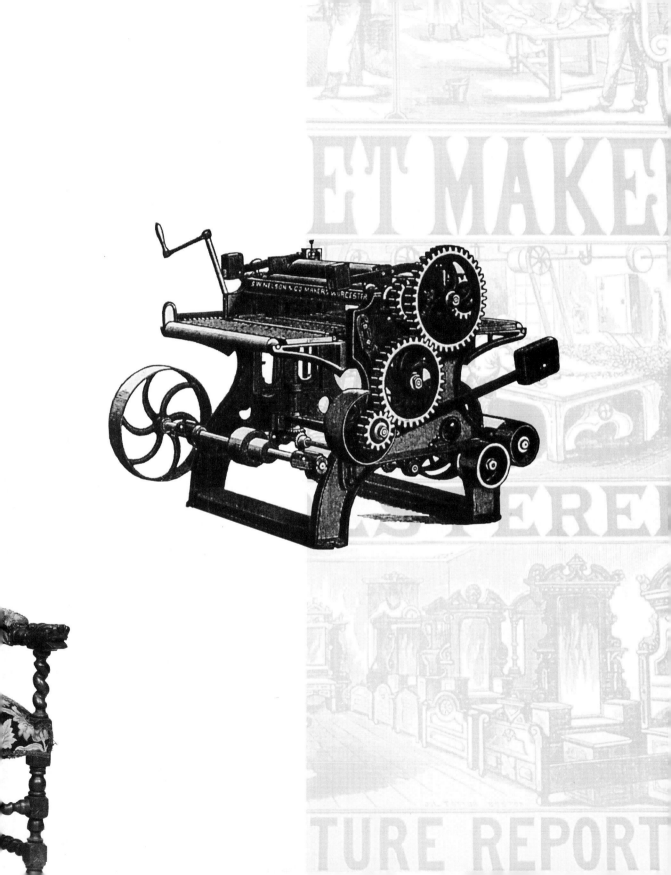

This dog-eared and yellowed centennial issue cover of the July 1, 1876, American Cabinetmaker, Upholsterer, and Furniture Reporter *vividly illustrates the remarkable technological progress brought about by the Industrial Revolution. Look closely because these pictures truly are worth a thousand words. In the center scene, water-powered jigs are being used to make multiple cuttings of decorative embellishment that will be applied to the furniture (see the bottom furniture showroom scenes), while at the top right, workers are hand-rubbing and shellacking headboards. This collage explains why some people say that the last quarter of the 19th century was a unique time, when technological advances and skilled labor worked hand in hand to create fine furniture.*

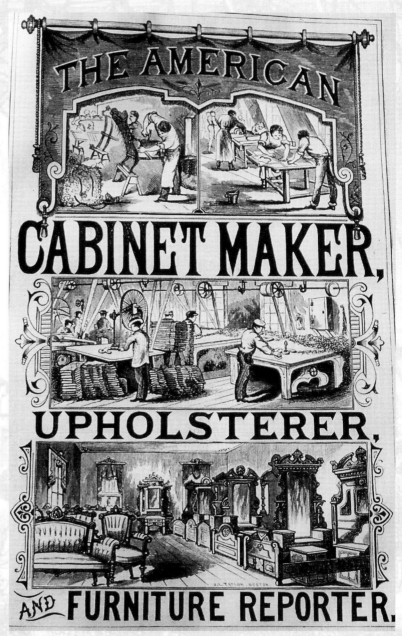

Though our ideas of comfort may change with the centuries, human dreams remain constant. The longing for a comfortable home to serve as a refuge from the toils of the workaday world was as real to the aspiring 1880s man as it is today.

chapter 1

The Coming of the Machine Age

When Grover Cleveland "touched the button" to turn on the electricity at the 1893 Columbian Exposition, he was symbolically ushering in a new era, one that would see machinery advance into the modern age.

The world was a rapidly changing place in the mid-nineteenth century. Cities were bursting at the seams. New democracies were springing up. Startling scientific and philosophical theories challenged old religious orders. And thanks to the telegraph, the railroad, and the steamship, the world was shrinking.

As Siegfried Giedion wrote in *Mechanization Takes Command,* "In the four decades from 1850 to 1890 no activity of everyday life was taken for granted. An unbridled inventive urge shaped everything anew." It was a time of new dreams, new possibilities.

The everyday American walking down Main Street, U.S.A., during the second half of the nineteenth century—man or woman—if asked his dreams or his personal aspirations replied it was to own a piece of land, to have a lovely house, and to fill it with tasteful furnishings—if not immediately, eventually. A remarkable number of these dreams, once attainable only by the well-to-do, would become a reality for the masses by the end of the century.

Wood, Water, and Lots of Machines

At the core of every major furniture manufacturing center there were two basic natural resources: wood and water. And machines.

"The machine is here to stay. It is the forerunner of the democracy that is our dearest hope," wrote Frank Lloyd Wright in *The Art and Craft of the Machine.*

The year was 1901, thirty-six years after the end of the Civil War, twenty-five years after the Philadelphia Centennial Exposition, and eight years after the 1893 Chicago Columbian Exposition.

By 1901 machines *were* here—machines of all types and in all phases of life. But the development of the American furniture industry during the 1850–1890 era that led up to the twentieth century was more than just the whirl of circular saws, lathes, mortising machines, and power-driven carving machines that duplicated hand carving in the factories of Williamsport, Massachusetts; Thomasville, North Carolina; Rockford, Illinois; and even Muscatine, Iowa.

The American furniture industry actually devel-

By the 1880s, a strong, nostalgic sense of the past was ever-present through romanticized Currier and Ives scenes that hung on the wall of every home, as well as views like this one taken from Clarence Cook's decorating bible of the time, The House Beautiful. *"Things Old and New," the caption reads, but we today must wonder which ones are old and which ones are new? What better evidence could there be that reproductions of the "olden days" were already a part of daily life?*

oped as a result of literally hundreds of inventions and technological advances ranging from gas lighting and steam-powered engines to the completion of the transcontinental railroad in 1869.

From Cottage Industry to Industrial Centers

Before the Civil War, most furniture was made in small towns, not large cities. From the earliest days of the nineteenth century, anywhere wood and water coexisted, hundreds of small furniture companies had sprung up in the fledgling United States. Just as the individual furniture maker or small workshop had done during the eighteenth century, so small craft shops, rather than major factories, supplied the furniture needs of local families. The later nineteenth century would change all this.

During the 1870s, in locations where there were clusters of these small shops, furniture centers began to develop, especially where good overland or water transportation to nearby urban areas was available. Ultimately, transportation systems that linked rich forests to major cities—first rivers and canals, then plank roads, and eventually railroads—were responsible for turning small crossroads towns into full-blown industrial manufacturing cities during the second half of the nineteenth century.

When the turmoil of the Civil War had quieted down, furniture manufacturing emerged as a viable national industry. Three major furniture-making centers soon developed: southwestern

> There is a fortune in store for any one who to-day will supply the public with well-made, well-designed furniture—well-designed both for beauty and use—at cheap rates. It can be done by first getting from competent hands designs that have been thoroughly thought out, reduced to their simplest elements, and so planned that they can be made in quantities.
>
> —CLARENCE COOK,
> *THE HOUSE BEAUTIFUL*, 1878

New York State, upper Michigan, and central and western North Carolina. By now, railroads linked these areas to the major cities of New York, Boston, Detroit, Pittsburgh, Atlanta, and New Orleans.

But a companion industry that had also made giant strides forward during the war years helped the blossoming of the furniture industry—the printing industry.

The Power of the Press

Today we take the powerful and interconnected influence of the mass media and pop culture in stride. (MTV says it all.) But this was a new concept in the nineteenth century when two innovative art-related business phenomena burst on the scene. They led the way, with the help of the printing press, for "popular art" to make its way into the hearts (for both of these art forms idealized the family) and homes of the public.

First came the well-known, mass-produced Currier and Ives prints that sold originally for a pittance and now can sell for thousands of dollars. These were so popular in the 1840s that a London office had to be established to accommodate the European clientele.

Then, a less-known today but then very famous American sculptor, John Rogers, created his "Rogers group" plaster statues. (A loose comparison might be drawn between his 1860s "Norman Rockwell–like groups" and the 1990s goods made by the Franklin Mint.) A brilliant marketer, the popular and successful Rogers reached his middle-class audience the same way many companies do today—by mail order.

The way was paved so that by the 1870s the newest furniture styles were made irresistible through mail-order catalogs featuring colored chromolithographs—the same printing process Currier and Ives had used. Striking pamphlets, magazine advertisements, and a rush of "lifestyle" books were filled with ideas on how to make your house beautiful.

Furthermore, the furniture being sold nationwide through mail-order catalogs was delivered from the factory to your town by railroad. In *Chicago Furniture,* Sharon Darling tells how, in 1878, a Pullman car was outfitted with two furniture showrooms and sent into the Western territories. Eventually though, this method was abandoned and furniture-store owners themselves rode the trains to the cities.

MANUFACTURED BY THE

KNAPP DOVETAILING MACHINE CO., FLORENCE, MASS.

This new machine is built to make two sizes of the "Knapp" joint, giving it a wide range of work; and in many other respects it is an improvement on the Knapp machine. Every part is made to gauge, so that duplicate parts, that will require no re-fitting or adjusting, can at all times be furnished for repairs.

WE ALSO CONTINUE TO MAKE THE

✦ ✦ **KNAPP DOVETAILING MACHINE,** ✦ ✦

Which for the last fifteen years has excelled all other Dovetailers in the rapidity of its operation [and the strength and beauty of its joint.

GRAND RAPIDS, MICH., Dec. 12, 1887.

The Knapp Dovetailer purchased of you six years ago has been in constant operation from the day it arrived. We have never spent anything on the machine for repairs, and in running same have turned out complete twenty-one hundred drawers in sixty hours. We regard the joint made by it the strongest and most perfect we have ever seen.

McCord & Bradford Furniture Co.,
F. R. Luce, Superintendent.

Catalogue A Wood Working Machinery
Catalogue C Power Transmitting Machinery

America's First True Furniture City

One city had all the necessary ingredients to become a great manufacturing center immediately after the Civil War: nearby natural resources, fine craftsmen, great railroad and shipping facilities, and an ever-expanding population all around it. This city was Chicago.

Chicago was well on its way to becoming the foremost furniture manufacturing center when the city was almost totally destroyed by the devastating fire of 1871.

Ironically, what at first appeared to be a major tragedy to her industries actually gave Chicago an edge over the rest of the country. The companies had to rebuild. When they did, old equipment was replaced with the most modern steam

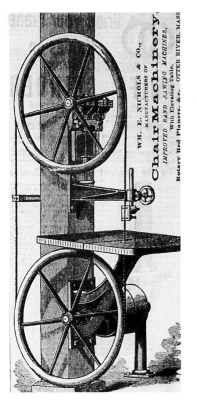

machinery. Companies elsewhere simply could not afford to scrap their still-functioning and perfectly adequate tools and equipment for the much more expensive, new power-driven models.

Meanwhile, in many parts of the country, human labor was still less expensive than buying and installing modern machinery. In those areas without adequate steam or water power to run the new machines, human labor was the only option. Eventually though, the competition from the Chicago furniture industry created a new industrial standard throughout the country.

So, by the end of the 1870s, an industry that had begun in small workshops in crossroads towns was now bringing style, fashion, and function into the homes of Americans across the country at a fraction of the cost and time it had taken only a few years earlier.

Just think, by this time, an entire suite of living room, dining room, or bedroom furniture could be made in less time than it had taken the eighteenth-century craftsman to produce just one piece of furniture by hand. By now manufactured furniture was being turned out by the boxcar load.

In the last quarter of the century the furniture industry was sufficiently large to support manufacturers of the new machines. By now, dovetailing and boring machines and band saws (opposite and above) were standard equipment in furniture workshops across the country.

In The American Cabinetmaker, Upholsterer, and Furniture Reporter *the furniture advertisements are for Victorian suites of furniture in the then-popular Renaissance Revival style. Might the cornice on the bed and dresser be the very one receiving the coat of shellac on the cover (page 2)? By now, machinery made it possible to create an entire suite of furniture in less time than it had taken 18th-century craftsmen to build just one piece.*

The Machine Meets the Craftsman

But there is more to making a piece of furniture than sawing boards and fitting drawers together. *Ornamentation*—carving, applying inlay, and so on—and the *finish*—loveliest when hand-rubbed—add interest and quality to each piece. Because these steps are often "mechanized" today, many people do not realize that much early reproduction furniture often combined manufacturing shortcuts with fine craftsmanship.

You see, the late nineteenth and early twentieth centuries were a special time in the history of American furniture. Wonderful craftsmen, carvers, finishers, and joiners who had learned their skills in Europe were flocking to America and bringing their specialized knowledge with them.

Simultaneously, new power-driven machines and equipment made such labor-intensive and time-consuming jobs as sawing and planing much simpler. Yet at this time many, if not most, of the steps necessary to produce a fine piece of furniture still required the talents of a skillful operator.

Remember, this is the end of the nineteenth century, not the

"CHAMPION."
Folding Bedstead & Crib,

THE BEST IN THE WORLD!
First Premium and Silver Medal
Awarded 1874.
FACTORIES
Nos. 48 & 50 North Sixth St.

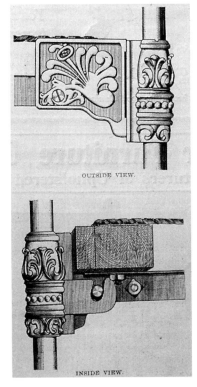

OUTSIDE VIEW.

INSIDE VIEW.

end of the twentieth century. In those days machines were largely controlled by precision movements of the operator's hand or foot, not by flicking a switch, pushing a button, or punching in instructions.

The *individually* operated lathe, mortising machine, and carving machines remained the mainstay of the furniture manufacturing companies. The hand-finishing of surfaces and carved decorations was definitely still required. Truly *automated* furniture production came slowly, one technological development building on another. Industry-wide automation was not in place until well into the second half of the twentieth century.

Though the Civil War brought many advances in machines, technology, and transportation, other important changes in manufacturing that we now take for granted did not come about until after World Wars I and II. (Isn't it interest-

All the while the machines were making production faster, new inventions made it possible to build both stronger and more innovative furniture. For those who needed extra room in their small quarters, the "folding bedstead and crib" (top) was the best in the world! But if you preferred a stationary bed, H. R. Doughtery & Co., makers of "faultless bedding," developed a better, more secure hook (left).

ing how scientific and technological revolutions often evolve from man's attempts to conquer the world!)

Taking a Second Look

And so, if yours is the mind-set that considers all manufactured furniture to be inferior to hand-crafted pieces, think again. Style, design, condition, quality, materials, construction—each of these elements is important when assessing a piece of furniture. *A poorly constructed eighteenth-century piece that is of displeasing design and made of poor-quality wood—even if every part is hand hewn and assembled—will be inferior to a well-constructed later reproduction that is a beautifully designed and styled piece made of choice woods.*

Old, but Not Old Enough

Over the years, reproduction furniture unfortunately has gotten a bad rap just because of that one word "machine-made." But look closer.

The concept that all "machine-made" furniture is inferior exists largely because the public knows next to nothing about the whole process of furniture construction.

For example, some of the same people who snub

> **No technological change had a more direct effect upon the family than the introduction of power machinery.**
>
> —ANTHONY N. B. GARVAN, "EFFECTS OF TECHNOLOGY ON DOMESTIC LIFE, 1830–1880," *TECHNOLOGY IN WESTERN CIVILIZATION*

"reproduction pieces" may be charmed by a late Victorian piece. What they do not know is that the late Victorian piece they think is so wonderful and call "antique" is just as much "machine-made" as is the reproduction piece they are snubbing. That is why knowing even just a little about furniture construction and assembly can be an eye-opener.

A detailed discussion of the word "antique" appears on page 11. Because people throw this word around so casually and intermix those definitions, many people assume that any piece called an antique is *handcrafted*. (That's the connoisseur's definition.) In reality, a piece of furniture may meet only the *grandmother* definition of an antique: a piece just has to be "old" to be called an antique.

So the problem comes when someone looks at a sixty-year-old Hepplewhite-style chair being called an "antique" and assumes the machine-cut, glued-on classical urn decoration at the back is hand carved, the way it was done in the eighteenth century. Our hypothetical shopper then buys the Hepplewhite-style chair and loves it . . . *until* someone tells him the difference between the eighteenth-century chair and his chair. Suddenly our friend's beloved chair becomes a "stepchild" when it should have been appreciated for itself all along.

Barnes Foot and Hand Power Machinery . . .
Scroll and Circular **Saws**, Mortisers, Formers, Tenoners, **Lathes**.
Send for Catalogue.
W. F. & JOHN BARNES CO., 570 Ruby Street, ROCKFORD, ILL.

Though the indispensable lathe was greatly improved during the last years of the 19th century, it still took skilled labor to operate this and other machines essential in the making of furniture.

Some furniture companies re-created classical styles like this "pretty table" that was clearly adapted from the "Duncan Phyfe" or transitional Sheraton/Empire period of just fifty or sixty years earlier. Interestingly, it was showcased in the same magazine as the innovative folding bedstead (page 8).

Nineteenth-Century Shortcuts

Where does this leave us? To avoid such mistakes, anyone interested in furniture styles and design should know these basic facts.

• Machine-cut dowels and dovetails were commonplace by the mid-nineteenth century. Even the finest Victorian furniture workshops that carved by hand the rich floral ornaments so highly prized by furniture connoisseurs used machines to cut dowels and dovetails.

• By the 1880s and 1890s, technology had developed machines that could simultaneously duplicate hand-carved motifs in multiple copies, while another machine could produce the effect of oak, rosewood, and other fine woods. That machine made it possible to make expensive-looking furniture out of cheaper woods.

• As for those machines that could make stacks of carved motifs that *seemingly* were made by hand one at a time, you must realize that craftsmen have *always* used dies, jigs, stencils, molds, templates, and patterns to make their out-

put consistent and efficient. That's just good business.

Ultimately, many of the processes that we look down upon and consider to be a part of "mass production" really are only labor-saving devices. Furthermore, making interchangeable furniture parts and constructing identical pieces on an assembly line is substantially different from robotic automation.

As the century drew to a close, the machines themselves began to take on a new look. Sleeker machines with greater strength, dependability, and efficiency guaranteed a better product for forward-looking companies poised to turn out the quantities of new furniture the public was demanding.

JUST HOW OLD IS IT?

I am often asked, "Just how old does something have to be to be an antique?" "It depends," I smilingly reply, for there are really three definitions, depending upon who answers the question.

The legal definition, one established by the U.S. Customs Service, requires that items entering the country as "antique," and therefore duty-free, must be one hundred years old. This means that each year, items made a hundred years earlier, which only the year before were just "old," may now be classified as antique.

Everyone agrees that this circa 1780 Philadelphia Chippendale chair has earned the right to be called an "antique," based on its age and craftsmanship. (Photo courtesy of Craig and Tarlton)

Almost everyone will agree that this fine mid-19th-century New York dresser should be called an antique, based on both its age and its quality. Yet some purists will object on the basis that many machines were used to make this piece, even though as has been explained, these machines required skilled workmen to operate them. (Photo by David Nicolay, courtesy of Neal Auction Company)

Connoisseurs often use the term "antique" only when referring to pieces handcrafted before the outset of the Industrial Revolution and the coming of the machine age, or approximately 1830 or 1840. This definition offends some people because it automatically excludes later Empire and all Victorian furniture, even that made in the 1840s and 1850s, now a century and a half ago.

There is yet another definition, and it is one that I don't particularly like. It defines an antique as anything that belonged to "Granny." Since I'm old enough to be a grandmother but hopefully am not yet an antique, I prefer to stick with the U.S. government's definition.

In these pages, an antique will refer to pieces one hundred or more years of age.

So what do we call this early-20th-century Adam-style sideboard? Its circa 1915 date eliminates it from legally being an antique until it is a full one hundred years old. For now it must be called an old reproduction. But soon it will be an antique for the next generation. (Photo by David Nicolay, courtesy of Neal Auction Company)

Machines: The Secret to Quickness and Quantity

In the introduction I apologized for not being able to include everything I wanted to in these pages. One area I wish there were room to expand on is the evolution of technology at the turn of the century. Yet I know many readers would skip over passages that get bogged down in the mechanics of making the furniture. Those readers are more interested in the look and the age of the pieces than in *how* they were made. Still, in many instances, *how* the furniture was made directly affected the way it looked, and tell-tale signs left by tools and machines are certainly clues to accurately dating a piece. So here, for those who are interested, is a brief summary, so to speak, that provides more, but not too much, information about tools and machines used in making furniture and the impact they have had through the years.

Everyone knows that rudimentary hand tools have always been used to make furniture. Engineers and craftsmen alike have sought to make their tools better, to improve both the equipment and the quality and appearance of the final product. But most of all they were seeking ways to reduce the amount of time it took to make each piece.

Giant steps toward this end were made throughout the seventeenth, eighteenth, and nineteenth centuries. Steam power gave men capabilities they had only dreamed of, and with the widespread use of electric power in the early twentieth century, the rate at which new inventions appeared reached fever pitch.

Scholars who read this book will delve deeper into the study of machine tools and their effect on furniture-making. These few pages are simply to acquaint others with some basics about tools and to lightly touch on the different types of work that the most common tools perform.

The 1990s have left the developments made at

"The first day I used the machine I got more out in half a day than I could have done in two days the old way," A. R. Young wrote in praise of the new machinery. Quickness has always been the motivating reason to improve tools; that's why Young added, "I shall want some other machines soon."

the turn of the century in a cloud of dust, as they say. But at the time, these changes in furniture-making were both remarkable and life-changing.

ASSEMBLY-LINE PRODUCTION

Even before the newfangled tools of the Industrial Revolution brought sweeping changes in the way furniture was made, innovative ways of organizing the work began making mass production easier.

In 1825, Lambert Hitchcock settled in what is now Riverton, Connecticut, a town where two rivers met. There he built a small furniture factory with the intention of mass-producing chairs based on a Sheraton design. To make the job go more efficiently, Hitchcock divided up the steps involved in making the chairs.

On the first floor of the factory, water-powered lathes, boring tools, and mortising machines were used to process lumber and bend, cut, and turn chair posts, legs, stretchers, and backsplats. On the second floor, these pieces were glued together and placed in drying kilns. When each part was ready, they were then finished, painted, and decorated with stencils. Soon this little factory was producing fifteen thousand chairs a year.

Meanwhile, in New York City, Duncan Phyfe found he could increase his workshop's output by dividing tasks between semi-skilled workmen, who did preparatory work on lathes and other machines, and skilled carvers, who finished the furniture the workmen had begun.

> To whom can this period of decadence in household art and architecture be attributed, if not to the pestilent inventor of the buzz-saw?
>
> —AN UNKNOWN SOCIAL CRITIC IN THE 1850s

FIRST, WATER POWER

The first "powered" tool to use energy other than human "elbow grease" was the water-powered lathe that came into use during the seventeenth century. Wheels powered by water and guided by either the hand or a foot pedal made the tedious job of cutting and shaping strips of wood much easier. By the end of the eighteenth century a number of similarly powered tools were in use.

In the furniture industry, though, the band saw—an endless toothed steel sheet that ran between two wheels—which was patented in England in the late 1700s, was the most important. About the same time, in 1775, John Wilkinson invented a water-powered guided borer. By the time Sir Mark Brunel invented the power veneer saw in 1805, and patented a different steam-powered slicing device which he described as "a method of cutting veneer by means of a horizontal knife exceeding in length the piece to be cut" in 1806, the making of furniture had been revolutionized.

Scroll saws, circular saws, molding machines, tenoning machines, and dovetailing machines were also introduced during the first quarter of the nineteenth century, and with each passing year minor improvements were made on each and every one of these wonderful new inventions. If they had one drawback, it was that their success or failure depended on the skill of the operator, for water-powered tools only assisted the operator in making his job go more quickly and easily.

For the most part these new tools were fairly quickly integrated into cabinetmaking shops and were in widespread use by the 1830s and 1840s. The band saw was the notable exception, because problems arose in developing a durable steel blade for it. But by the late 1850s this invaluable time-saver was in place in the larger cabinetmakers' shops.

In particular, these machines dramatically improved productivity:

• *circular saws* enabled a woodworker to obtain twice the number of veneers from the same block of wood in half the time hand sawing required

• *scroll saws* greatly simplified the cutting of irregular patterns, especially those required by the popular Gothic style

• *band saws* allowed for the standardized production of curved forms such as couch legs, feet, and arm supports that could be stored until they were required for finishing or assembly

• *foot-powered mortising machines* drastically reduced the amount of time involved in joining chair parts because the strong mortise and tenon joints were guaranteed not to need touching up

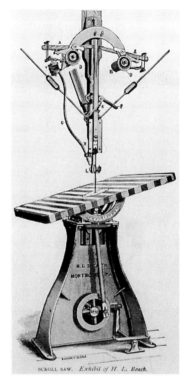

SCROLL SAW. *Exhibit of H. L. Beach.*

By the end of the century a dependable scroll saw was considered essential in the furniture workshop of any size.

First, a cabinetmaker's financial ability to invest in new machines, not to mention the requisite power plant, was often a huge stumbling block. Even if a particular cabinetmaker's products were in demand and he had a fairly large operation, location on or near a constant source of water was a necessity.

Next, the shop had to have access to a good transportation system—in those days either a waterway or a railroad. It wouldn't do him any good to make the furniture if he couldn't ship it to other cities, since his production would surpass demand in the immediate area before too long.

For the man with dreams of great expansion, often his small cabinet shop was not large enough to accommodate the massive steam-powered machinery. But for the average, smaller cabinetmaker, happy to serve only his general region, this was not so important. By now lumber mills were inexpensively mass-producing uniform moldings, turnings, and rough stock as well as veneers suitable for furniture manufacturing. Some cabinetmakers even sent out their own wood to be rough hewn at nearby lumber mills.

NEXT, STEAM POWER

Fast on the heels of water power was steam power, but furniture workshops found adapting to this new type of power was a much slower process because of many factors.

THE BIG PICTURE

Competition was an ever-growing threat. Some companies, especially those in the East, were rapidly growing thanks to the continuing improvements in technology as shown by the following case history, researched by Jan Seidler and included in the book *Tools and Technology.*

In 1817, Thomas Smallwood, an English immigrant and cabinet-maker, set up a small but thriving business near Boston in Charlestown. His tradecard advertised furniture in the newest neoclassical style, leaving us to surmise that his products were available to the

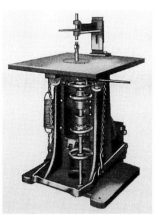

Competition also loomed in the background when the 20th century introduced technologically advanced equipment that combined several jobs in one tool but also often forced the closing of small operations that could not change with the times.

wealthy buyers who could afford the latest fashion. He most likely employed five to ten master journeymen and apprentices and outside, or contract, craftsmen to do specialized jobs.

By the late 1840s, his son Edwin was in charge of the business. Edwin abandoned the Charlestown shop for a steam-powered factory in Newton, Massachusetts, where he employed fifty to seventy-five workmen and mass-produced black walnut and mahogany parlor suites. Edwin was a shrewd marketer and set up showrooms in Boston, where, by the 1860s, railroads could take his furniture west and ships could take it abroad. Special lines without veneer (which might warp or crack) were designed for export to places as

far away as Australia, Venezuela, and the Sandwich Islands.

Imagine growing from a small workshop to an internationally known manufacturer in one generation in the 1800s. Smallwood's story is not unusual. This is how fortunes were made, and technology made it all possible.

Indeed, by the 1850s, cabinetmaking and related crafts and industries represented a crucial part of New England's industrial economy, and continued to be just that through most of the century. Yet not everyone everywhere was so quick to change, as Polly Anne Earl discussed at the 1973 Winterthur conference, *Technological Innovation and the Decorative Arts.*

New Castle County, Delaware, which is in close proximity to Philadelphia, one of the nation's earliest hotbeds of steam technology, had no cabinetmakers using steam or water power as late as 1870, even though 70 percent of the lumber milling establishments in the county were by then using steam power to make doors, blinds, and other products.

By the first years of the 20th century, it seemed the days when accomplished local craftsmen could satisfy their customers with well-turned and practical chairs would be gone forever. But in reaction to the machine age (above), men like Wallace Nutting revived the craft by creating fine-quality reproductions using 18th-century models and methods (below). (Photo courtesy of Michael Ivankovich)

Yet Cincinnati, an early Midwestern center for furniture manufacturing, took advantage of the westward expansion of the young nation *and* its river access to markets in the South. In 1850, Cincinnati had sixty-one furniture manufacturing firms. Seventeen, or 27.8 percent, of them employed steam, water, or horse power. That number jumped to 54.5 percent in 1870. In 1890, at the zenith of its power as a furniture center, Cincinnati had 130 furniture-making establishments and three thousand people were employed in the industry. Before the end of the century, Cincinnati had been eclipsed by Chicago and especially by Grand Rapids, Michigan, where in 1870 there were eight businesses employing 281 people but in 1910 there were fifty-four businesses employing 7,254 people.

SPEED AND PROFITABILITY

During the last years of the century, the ultimate goal of furniture manufacturers was not complete automation. Rather, it was to increase profits and productivity. They did this by eliminating as many of the tedious and labor-intensive hand processes as possible and replacing them with machine processes.

The old way had changed. Gone was much of the creative joy the craftsmen of old had known. Craftsmen now were needed only to add the ornamental touches—carving, painting, gilding, finishing—to each piece.

One outgrowth of the furniture industry was the trade papers. By the 1890s their pages were filled with manufacturers' advertisements and reports on the new models of machinery that would improve the factories even more. Not only were the machines getting faster and faster, they were cutting *uniform* parts, like doors and

THE RIGHT NAME

Much confusion can occur when trying to identify pieces of furniture that look the same on the outside but were made at different times.

Chair A, below, was made circa 1780. Chair B, right, was made circa 1880–1883 by the Sypher Company of New York City. Chair C, bottom, was made circa 1916. Chairs A and B can *legally* be called "antiques," yet chair A is a hundred years older than chair B. How do you distinguish between them? It is done by using two words: "period" and "style."

PERIOD, in antiques language, denotes that a piece was made during the *original time* when the design became popular. Therefore, chair A is properly referred to as a "*period* Chippendale chair."

STYLE, in antiques language, denotes that a piece is in the fashion or nature of an earlier period but made *at a later time.*

Chair B must therefore be called a Chippendale-*style* chair, even though it is legally an antique.

Still, chair B is approximately forty years older than chair C. Though both chairs B and C were manufactured rather than handcrafted, many people feel that those forty years are important and want to know the age each piece. That's when the use of the term "circa" (often abbreviated as c. or ca.) becomes important.

CIRCA means about, or approximately. In antiques language, circa covers an approximate twenty-to-thirty-year time span. The spread refers to ten or fifteen years on each side of an identifying, signature date. For example, circa 1800 would cover the time span from 1785 to 1815.

Circa is a logical and important age denotation because it seldom can be known positively that a piece was made in, say, 1750. It might have been made in 1748 or 1756.

Even manufactured pieces, though often signed, are seldom dated. Who can tell if a Baker reproduction chest of drawers was made in 1907 or 1920? In a word, "circa" is a benchmark date.

B

A

(Photo A courtesy of Craig and Tarlton; photo B courtesy of the Rhode Island School of Design, Museum of Art, Gift of Commander William Davis Miller)

C

drawer fronts, even dovetails, that were interchangeable on different furniture forms. What better evidence could there be that machines were the real power behind the furniture industry? Polly Anne Earl summed it up by explaining that in 1898 the machine-made parts of a sideboard could be fitted together in 18 hours—a job that had taken 210 hours to assemble a hundred years before.

And more changes were just around the corner. Once the switch was flipped and electrical power turned on the machines, mechanization and motion were wedded—a marriage that would last for almost a century, until the 1990s and the beginning of a whole generation of new changes brought about by computer technology that we, like our ancestors of the 1890s, still can barely fathom.

Reproductions Made on the Other Side of the Ocean

Meanwhile, in Europe it didn't take long for the French to regret the wholesale disposal at the end of the French Revolution of the luxurious and exquisite furniture that had adorned the palaces and aristocratic homes of the noblemen. Once things quieted down and the French merchant and banking industries gave rise to a wealthy and tasteful middle class, guess what? *They* wanted the trappings that the wealthy seemingly always want: the finest and most beautiful furnishings money can buy. When they looked around at the style of the day—Empire and Directoire—and the styles from the past—the Louis—the past won, hands down.

In Paris alone, thousands of men worked to create copies of the 18th-century furniture masterpieces that had been destroyed as a result of the French Revolution. These 1885 scenes show the interior of a bustling Parisian factory. (Photos courtesy of the Antique Collectors' Club)

In no time at all the furniture makers were once again turning out the Louis XV and XVI styles that only a short while before had been discarded. Only this time the work was not in the ateliers of the *ébénistes* (workshops of the finest craftsmen). Now the pieces were coming out of large furniture factories. Christopher Payne points out in his masterly work *Price Guide to 19th-Century European Furniture* that in Paris alone (in the 1830–1840 era a city of over a million people), the furniture retail business supported 1,200 employees, and the manufacturing industry another 17,000.

And so, as in America, also in France and England, Payne writes: "The industrial age of steam driven saws and veneer knives was fully equipped to deal with this unprecedented demand for furniture. Every household wanted and was able to buy more pieces than might be strictly necessary and by the middle of the century the move to overfurnishing . . . was well under way."

But as more and more furniture was turned out faster and faster, the quality of the end products varied greatly. Payne cites that by the 1880s perhaps 2,000 men were employed in the furniture industry to make *meubles de luxe* (the very finest gilded furniture), while 14,500 men were making less expensive *meubles courant* (furniture for the masses).

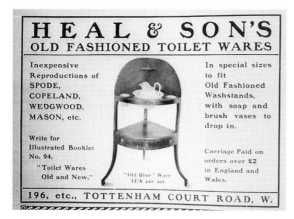

In England, reproduction furniture seems to have been around forever. Here, from a 1904 Connoisseur *magazine, is an ad for reproduction china made to fit in "old-fashioned" washstands. I'll wager many of those old-fashioned washstands were as new as the china (below).*

It goes without saying that the reproduction furniture made during this era outnumbered hundreds and thousands of times the amount of existing *period* Louis XV and XVI furniture. Remember, by now it took less time to create the furniture to furnish an entire room than it had taken to make just one chair in the eighteenth century. It also goes without saying that the new middle class, in their rush to get "look-alikes" of the early style, took what the manufacturers gave them. The furniture designers most often took the concept of the early, period styles and adapted them to the new times and the new machines.

Just as newly rich American industrialists like Seiberling and McFaddin (see page

I'd hate for readers who believe every "18th-century" label on a piece of English furniture to see this little pamphlet that I picked up twenty-plus years ago in a used-book store. In the early 1900s quaint English shops were already advertising and carrying reproduction 18th-century furniture which, after it passed through a few hands, lost its modern birthright and suddenly became "antique." The "antique-appearing" Welsh dressers are all reproductions.

58), who were making their money from the new machines, thought machine-made furniture was the best, so Payne explains that in France "there was an undoubted feeling of pride in the achievement of production. After all man had made the machines to make the furniture and thus was able to make more of it to satisfy the immensely expanding market."

Meanwhile, the same thing was happening in England. By the 1860s the English furniture industry was turning out untold numbers of reproductions based on their country's earlier styles—Jacobean, Queen Anne, Chippendale, Adam, Hepplewhite, and to a lesser degree Sheraton. John Andrews, in his book *The Price Guide to Victorian, Edwardian and 1920s Furniture,* writes how, from 1860 onward, there "was the mass-produced and craftsman's furniture made in antiquarian styles," and how by the end of World War I, "the easiest thing [for the furniture makers] to do was to rely on the 18th century."

The huge quantities of these "adaptations" make up the majority of European and English furniture on the marketplace today. But of course, many of these adaptations are often mislabeled "eighteenth century" and are sold as period antiques.

Chapters 6 and 7 go into the differences between period and reproduction furniture and how the earlier styles were adapted to nineteenth- and twentieth-century homes and lifestyles. But at this point, knowing how, why, and how many of English and French reproductions were made certainly will make you more astute, and even more appreciative of the quality of much of this output. You see, if these pieces can be passed off as "eighteenth-century antiques," they must have much to commend them!

The Most Important Criterion

I love antiques. To me there is nothing more beautiful than a handcrafted, well-designed eighteenth-century piece of furniture made from richly grained wood.

But not everyone can have that piece. Not everyone wants that piece. Not everyone can afford that piece. That is why, once *quality* is acknowledged to be the single most important criterion by which to judge the worth of a piece, and it is recognized that many hand processes were used in making early fine reproduction furniture, we can hope that *well-made* reproduction pieces can stand on their own merits.

The old saw goes that the proof of the cook is in the pudding. The machine manufacturers must have patted themselves on the back when furniture companies like St. John's bragged that the labor-saving table-making machine was the backing that guaranteed "good tables to the user."

1851-1926

A KIMBEL & SON Inc.
15 East 60th Street
New York

THE SUAVE SEVENTIES

In the exhibit will be found the representation of a very elegant
and artistic cabinet, one of the finest specimens of the furniture
designer's art. The closest scrutiny can detect no blemish in its
mechanical finish, while the general design is strikingly beautiful
and effective. The space where this elegant piece of furniture is
displayed was so thronged by admiring visitors that the exhibi-
tors were obliged to protect it with ropes and all excepting a
favored few had to content themselves with viewing it from a
distance by the aid of magnifying glasses.

WE quote Harper's Weekly for December, 1876, from an article on the
furniture displays at the Centennial Exposition, and illustrate above
our own exhibit there, when we were already a quarter of a century old.
It will amaze some of our readers, the interest shown even at
that early era in the decoration of interiors. But they will be even more
astounded at the furniture and interiors themselves, about which, in the seventies, they wrote so suavely.
A glance at the costumes of that fantastic period, with their flounces, their
waterfalls, their appliqué and insertions; yes, even the bang and chignon
under the absurd bonnets, invites comparison with the over-ornamented, over-
carved and witless meaningless designs of their contemporary interior decoration.

ANTIQUES   REPRODUCTIONS   FABRICS

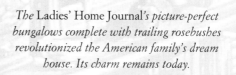

The Ladies' Home Journal's *picture-perfect
bungalows complete with trailing rosebushes
revolutionized the American family's dream
house. Its charm remains today.*

*Even years after the Centennial Exhibition, its
influence continued to be felt. In the March
1926 issue of* International Studio *magazine,
A. Kimbel & Son of New York placed this ad—
an illustration and quote from the December
1876 issue of* Harper's Weekly—*showing
Kimbel's exhibit at the Exhibition. At the
exhibit, Kimbel wrote, "[W]e were already a
quarter of a century old. . . . It will amaze some
of our readers, the interest shown even at that
early era in the decoration of interiors."*

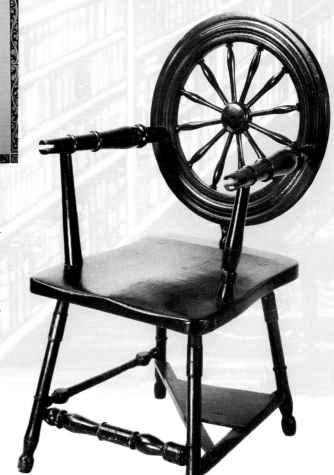

chapter 2

The New Styles

The Changing Scene

Factories weren't the only places where changes were taking place during the last half of the nineteenth century. Changes were rapidly invading every aspect of life at home as well, from the division of labor within the home to the books and magazines everyone was reading.

While some of these changes can be traced to the new scientific and technological advances of the day—iron ranges in the kitchen and electric lamps in the parlor, for example—others had their roots in history and sentiment. It was, after all, the end of a century, a time when people traditionally glorify the past.

This romanticizing of bygone days created a longing in people for furniture that looked like the pieces their ancestors had had. The new technology made it possible for them to have it.

In houses all across the United States, heavily carved horsehair-upholstered parlor suites that only a few years earlier had been the fashion rage were now hauled up to the attic. Down

Everyone who writes about this era includes reference to this "spinning wheel" chair (opposite) made c. 1886. No other symbol captures quite so vividly the nostalgia for the 18th century. (Photo courtesy of the Rhode Island School of Design, Museum of Art)

The Centennial Exhibition of 1876, fittingly held in Philadelphia, showcased the latest Victorian styles made by the most modern machinery. But when the visitors saw "Colonial" scenes re-created, the stage was set for a revival in interest in "the olden times."

came the pieces that had been cast off by previous generations—a mahogany Queen Anne tea table, a cherry Chippendale secretary, a pair of shield-back Hepplewhite side chairs. If you didn't have these to bring down, you went out and bought them, or ones that looked like them.

How Life-Altering Changes Came About

What created this change in people's tastes? As it took an entire chain of new inventions and technology to create the furniture factories, so numerous interlinking cultural changes and events occurred that made the old furniture styles once again both attractive and desirable.

The Centennial Exhibition of 1876 was one such event. Visitors from across the country who flocked by railroad to Philadelphia were enthralled by the exposition's glorification of eighteenth-century American life. When they saw

such quaint exhibits as "A New England Kitchen" and "Log Cabin in 'Ye Olden Times,'" they longed to recapture the simpler, more "idyllic" life of Colonial America in their own homes.

For many people living in a Victorian home with knickknacks on every shelf, cut-velvet upholstered and foliage-carved parlor sets, opulent flowered draperies held back by braided roping, multitiered ebonized étagères, and an array of fern stands, floor-to-ceiling mirrors, and carved picture frames everywhere they turned, the change was welcome. Sturdy, simple Windsor chairs, graceful but unadorned Chippendale serpentine-front desks, and the always nostalgic spinning wheel surely must have seemed like a breath of fresh air.

Interestingly, though, the exhibits at the famed Centennial Exhibition did not feature new furniture in the old styles. Rather, the manufacturers showcased the pieces currently in vogue—conventional chests and chairs, bookcases and tables in Eastlake (see page 32), "Modern" Gothic, and

Renaissance Revival styles—along with innovative "patent" furniture—folding chairs, hideaway beds, even Thonet designs (see page 30).

The Always Irresistible Good Old Days

Yet the old-fashioned, historical vignettes of irresistible kitchen and log cabin scenes complete with open hearths and spinning wheels sparked a nostalgic longing among the masses who saw them. If only the spirit, if not the actual day-to-day life, of that bygone era could be recaptured!

Even before reproduction furniture made its grand debut, many people who didn't have any of Granny's "old things" to bring down from the attic began scouring the countryside for *other people's* "old things." Soon pieces that had been considered cast-off furniture became valued antiques and a symbol of social status and old-family lineage.

An article in an 1897 furniture trade journal explained that everyone *now* regretted throwing away their old pieces. These days, the author wrote, "they are to be brought out and given places of honor in the house, eloquent illustrations of the survival as well as final appreciation of the fittest."

Astute furniture companies wasted no time capitalizing on this new trend. In their 1885 promotional pamphlet, "The Housekeeper's Quest: Where to Find Pretty Things," The Messrs.

A change is coming over the spirit of our time, which has its origin partly, no doubt, in the memorial epoch through which we are passing, but which is also a proof that our taste is getting a root in a healthier and more native soil. All this resuscitation of "old furniture" and revival of old simplicity (more marked, perhaps, in the east than here in New-York) is in reality much more sensible than it seems to be to those who look upon it as only another phase of the "centennial" mania.

—CLARENCE COOK, *THE HOUSE BEAUTIFUL*, 1878

Sypher and Company, a New York firm, advertised "copies of these old pieces (Chippendale, etc.) which are every way as handsome and well made as the originals, and so far as interior finish is concerned, [our] copies are often much better than their models."

The Philadelphia Centennial Exposition created such an interest in "Colonial-style" furnishings and styles that other exhibits soon followed.

In 1886, the New York Bicentennial Loan Exhibition, the first exhibit to assemble antique pieces from across the country, was held in Albany. Three years later, in 1889, the centennial celebrations of George Washington's inauguration brought a new rush of national pride and interest in Mount Vernon and its furnishings, as well as other historic homes.

The Old Country, a Step Ahead

This awareness of history was not confined to our American heritage; Americans were also increasingly aware of European culture.

The second half of the nineteenth century was a time of tremendous immigration to the United States from Europe, an important source for skilled craftsmen who worked in the furniture industry. Though immigrating families were seeking a better life in the United States, they brought their "old-world" likes and customs with them.

EDWARD BOK, DREAM WEAVER

While almost everyone is familiar with the *Ladies' Home Journal,* few people have ever heard of Edward Bok, its founder. Ironically, Bok's influence on our grandmothers' and great-grandmothers' taste in home furnishings and interior design was as far-reaching as Martha Stewart's influence is on the present generation.

A poor Dutch immigrant, Edward Bok untiringly campaigned for an improved standard of living in the place where he thought he could have the greatest effect: a down-to-earth but uplifting magazine for women. Bok's dream was for every family to have the best they could afford, especially a comfortable, livable home. To this end he published basic, no-frills house plans in the pages of the *Journal.*

It was only the 1890s, but already included in Bok's revolutionary ideas was the elimination of the formal "parlor" and its obligatory fireplace. He reasoned that the new, technologically advanced stoves and furnaces eliminated the need for the fireplace, and that the parlor was a needless frill.

When his house plans met with overwhelming popularity, Bok turned his magazine's attention to the interior of the home. In this subtle way, Bok heightened the American woman's pride in her turn-of-the-century role as the heart of the home and the selector of its furnishings. Today that image may seem idealized and even meet with criticism, but at the time Bok championed the American housewife's responsible role in life to give her a heightened sense of importance.

Recalling those years, Bok later wrote, "There are undoubtedly acute problems which concern themselves with the proper ingredients in cooking recipes, the correct stitch in crocheting or knitting . . . and the momentous question whether a skirt should escape the ground by six or eight inches. These are vital points in the lives of thousands of women, and their wisest solutions should be given by the best authorities." To that end, famous authorities of the day gave advice on home furnishings in the popular *Journal* features "Inside a Hundred Homes" and "Good Taste and Bad Taste."

By mixing instruction with inspiration, Bok, through his mouthpiece the *Ladies' Home Journal,* campaigned for women's suffrage, clean towns, wildlife conservation, better public health (his refusal to run ads for patent medicine led to the Pure Food and Drug Act in 1906), and homes decorated with the best-quality furnishings a family could afford—a dream still cherished in the 1990s by readers of the *Journal.*

An often forgotten, but very important, influence on American taste was the memory of Europe that immigrants brought with them to their new home. Combine this with the sights gathered by wealthy Americans on their "grand tour" of Europe and you immediately understand America's fascination with European furnishings. This 1916 scene shows an American bedroom suite made in Grand Rapids, Michigan, but in the Louis XV style.

Thus it was that European styles and fashions would greatly influence America's cultural life.

THE FRENCH CONNECTION

As significant as America's Civil War were the long Napoleonic Wars in Europe, which lasted from 1793 to 1815, years that also coincided with and hastened the development of the European Industrial Revolution. By the 1830s, throughout England and Europe, a heightened interest in the past flourished, spurred on by a combination of peace, expanded manufacturing capabilities, and the romantic influences of such writers as Scott, Tennyson, Balzac, and Goethe; such artists as Turner and Delacroix; and such composers as Berlioz and Mendelssohn. Throughout Europe, the 1840–1880 era brought a particularly renewed interest in French furniture, an interest that spread to America.

Over a hundred years earlier, when Louis XIV created the wondrous palace at Versailles in the late seventeenth century, French furniture became the epitome of style, design, and craftsmanship throughout Europe. Inspired by the "French look," eighteenth-century craftsmen in other countries instantly adapted the lines and opulence of this furniture to suit their own purposes, materials, and lifestyles.

On this side of the ocean though, American eighteenth-century furniture was most strongly influenced by English styles. Other than New Orleans, and to a lesser degree Savannah, America's major cities—Boston, New York, Philadelphia, Baltimore—were English-oriented. But by the mid-nineteenth century, the American furniture industry was doing what the Europeans had been doing for years: creating reproductions of Louis XIV, Louis XV, and Louis XVI furniture.

TAKING LIBERTIES WITH PERIOD STYLES

The appealing "French look" was rapidly embraced by Americans—both the wealthy and the middle class—and soon found its way into homes across the country. To complement the size and style of the American nineteenth-century home, the original eighteenth-century French lines, dimensions, and overall look of this elegant furniture underwent many changes in the hands of the American furniture designer. In fact, once the demand for reproductions of earlier-styled furniture took hold, *all* of the original eighteenth-century styles—French, English, even American furniture designs—underwent many adaptive changes. (These changes are further discussed and illustrated in Part Two.)

Eighteenth-century French, American, and of course English furniture styles dominated the burgeoning reproduction furniture industry in the United States, but German, Italian, Spanish, and northern European designs were also copied and adapted to nineteenth-century lifestyles.

The "Modern" Look

This is not to say that during the later nineteenth century the American public was interested only in its own and European *eighteenth-century*-style

For the young couple beginning to set up housekeeping on their own in the late 1880s and early 1890s, the Joseph Peters Furniture Company of St. Louis provided affordable Eastlake-influenced furniture with an "imitation walnut finish."

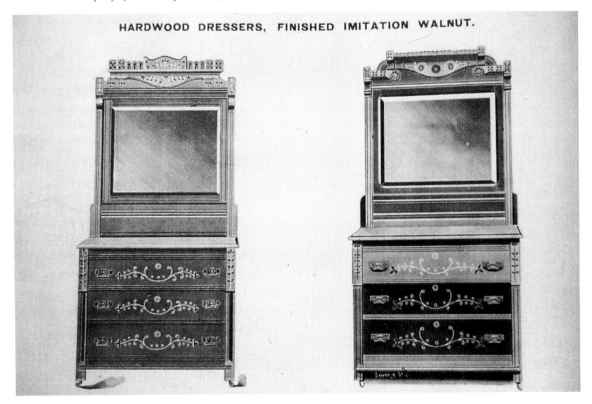

HARDWOOD DRESSERS, FINISHED IMITATION WALNUT.

Golden oak, that boldly grained wood that became fashioned into a distinct style as strong as the wood it was made of, led all furniture sales at the turn of the century.

These days, walnut, mahogany, cherry, and, to a lesser degree, maple are the preferred woods, while golden oak is looked down upon. But to the rising middle-class family at the end of the nineteenth century, oak was a wonderful wood. Visually, its natural dark stripes running through the blond wood gave oak a look all its own. Physically, this hardwood was strong and sturdy. Oak took wear and tear well, not to mention abuse. It was plentiful. It was solid, like the idealized American character of the era.

Furniture manufacturers turned oak furniture out by the gross. It was sold in stores, by mail order, and even became the basis of that American enterprise Larkin Premiums, whereby customers could cash in coupons they accumulated when buying Larkin products, from soap to jellies, for home furnishings.

In fact, when Golden Oak became

SAWED AND SLICED
Quartered
White Oak Veneers
INDIANA STOCK

Variety of Figure in
QUARTERED OAK VENEER
AS MANUFACTURED BY THE
Indiana Lumber
and Veneer Co.
INDIANAPOLIS, IND., U. S. A.
BRANCHES CARRYING COMPLETE STOCKS
Grand Rapids, Mich.: 89 Campau St.: Chas. McQuewan, Agent
New York, N. Y.: N. Y. Furniture Exchange: L. P. Hollowell, Agent

the mainstay of Sears and Montgomery Ward, these syndicate stores bought the "rights" to the Golden Oak furniture lines produced by many furniture companies, leaving the companies' other lines to be featured in the independent local furniture stores and advertised in the home-decorating magazines. This explains why there are few advertisements for Golden Oak furniture in the women's magazines of the early twentieth century.

But how do you describe its style? You can't, because Golden Oak pieces were made in a variety of designs loosely adapted from Queen Anne to Empire styling. Furthermore, the designs used by the Arts and Crafts artisans of the day were often picked up by the furniture manufacturers, who mass-produced similar-looking pieces in Golden Oak.

Because original eighteenth- and early-nineteenth-century furniture designs were *never* made of this wood, even those Golden Oak pieces that may look similar to some of the classical designs are not classified as "reproduction furniture."

Golden Oak furniture is recognized and called by its wood grain alone, rather than by any style or design of the piece. Clearly, this table base with its cabriole-type legs is loosely based on the Queen Anne lines of the 18th century, which illustrates the growing demand for pieces having a traditional look even though they were made for the "new" generation.

THONET'S BENTWOOD FURNITURE

There was nothing new about bending wood to fashion furniture parts. It had long been used in making everything from carriages to Windsor chairs to ships. Michael Thonet, an Austrian craftsman, brought the technique out of the workshop and into the furniture factory.

To produce vast quantities of bentwood furniture Thonet boiled strong poles of beechwood and then bent them into the appropriate shapes. These were then dried in ovens until the wood retained its new form. This basic technique eliminated the need for skilled craftsmen, and by creating the chairs in sections, they could be shipped unassembled and then screwed together upon delivery at the store. Though widely used in public places from waiting rooms to shipboard, Thonet chairs, benches, small tables, settees, and rockers were also found in middle-class homes.

When exhibited at the Philadelphia Centennial Exposition, Thonet's furniture offered the middle class a new look in mass-produced furniture. The furniture was handsome, "modern" in style, made by innovative manufacturing techniques, composed of only a few easily assembled parts, and, best of all, affordable. It was an instant hit with the public.

Aesthetically speaking, the design of Thonet furniture set it apart from the other furniture styles of the time. Historically speaking, it proved how important the use of modern techniques was becoming in the mass production of furniture in the 1870s.

furniture. Far from it. In the 1870s and 1880s the *newest modern* style sweeping the country was Eastlake furniture (see page 32).

Based on the ideas and designs presented in *Hints on Household Taste,* a book written by the Englishman Charles L. Eastlake in 1868, "Eastlake" furniture called for solid, simple, orderly, and functional furniture—quite in contrast to the ornate, cumbersome, and often frivolously ornamental Victorian style that immediately preceded it. Furthermore, Eastlake furniture was economically priced, a matter of great consideration, especially to younger couples.

A Place of Their Own

By the 1870s and 1880s, newlyweds were beginning to set up housekeeping, not with their parents (as had often been the way in the past) but in separate quarters—apartments in the larger cities where so many people were moving. Even those remaining in their smaller hometowns often began married life in rooming houses.

Everyone knows that each generation has its own fashion. Why should the young couple of the 1880s want furniture like their parents had? Remember, "parents have atrocious taste!"

These young couples, wanting to furnish their new homes, visited not the craftsman's shop but that new business, the furniture store. There they saw "Colonial," "European," and "Eastlake" pieces displayed side by side. The public now had a choice of styles to suit various tastes, and thanks to new technology and machines, a choice of quality to suit various budgets.

At the same time, another important new trend was developing on the horizon: small, livable, and affordable houses for growing families.

No proponent of *this* American dream was more influential than the *Ladies' Home Journal.*

The Bungalow for Main Street, U.S.A.

In the 1870s and 1880s the reigning fashion was Victorian- and Queen Anne–style homes trimmed with expensive frills—turrets, towers, porches, scalloped borders, turned spindles, ornamental balconies, and filigree work. These showplaces were hardly within reach of that growing segment of society of the 1890s, the

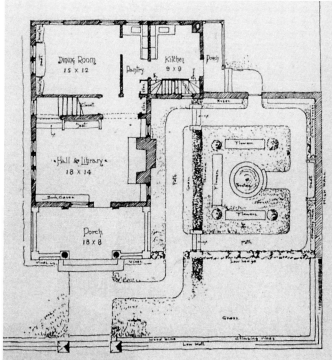

OF FIRST FLOOR AND GARDEN.

The house plans at the turn of the century may not seem so small to us now, but remember, the Victorian houses of just a few years earlier were spacious and rambling by comparison—and unaffordable for most.

EASTLAKE FURNITURE, 1870–1890

Charles Locke Eastlake, an Englishman, led the populist movement away from ornate, curvaceous Victorian furniture toward simpler, geometric designs on both sides of the Atlantic.

This concept of making furniture more functional by using straight lines and getting rid of superfluous ornamentation was only one component of an entire mid-nineteenth-century philosophical movement that advocated a return to "sincerity" in all phases of life. Frivolity and excessiveness in home furnishing and decorations as expressed by yards of damask, layers of ruffles, and borders of braided fringe was seen as physical evidence of a highly overindulgent lifestyle.

This was not a new idea. Years before, many critics spoke out about the frilly, poorly constructed "French-style" English copies displayed at the 1851 great Crystal Palace Exhibition. John Ruskin, the English philosopher, had already set forth this theory in his writings. A few years later, William Morris, another great proponent of simple design and sturdily constructed furniture, led the English Arts and Crafts Movement. But Eastlake's 1868 book *Hints on Household Taste* was the vehicle that introduced these philosophical concepts into the home in layman's terms.

This book was more than a philosophical treatise. It also provided advice on home decoration. In its pages the conscientious wife found guidance on furniture, wallpaper, carpeting, draperies, and decorative accessories. There were even illustrations of the new furniture styles.

Eastlake objected to Victorian furniture that had carving placed so that a "knotted lump of wood" became "inconvenient to the touch." So, to achieve the ideal combination of beauty and function, Eastlake reached back in history to Medieval designs and styles. The result was simple, "honest," and

(Photo courtesy of Greenwich Auction Room)

well-constructed properly designed furniture for the middle-class home.

In short, Eastlake adapted the rectilinear lines of Gothic-period furniture to nineteenth-century life. To break the starkness of the lines he added turned spindles, incised carving, and panels—all decorative ornaments of the Medieval time.

On surfaces usually decorated with high-relief Victorian-type carving, Eastlake used marquetry instead. "It is a pity that marquetry should have fallen into such disuse, for it is a very effective and not necessarily expensive mode of ornament," he wrote. "It consists of inlaying the surface of one wood with small pieces of another, differing from it in vein or color. These pieces will either be grouped in geometrical pattern, or arranged so as to represent natural objects conventionally."

Philosophically as well as aesthetically, Charles Eastlake objected to machine-carved ornamentation. He considered fine craftsmanship and excellent furniture construction necessary to returning "sincerity" to furniture. Yet he did not condemn the use of machinery. After all, the new machines of the era made it possible to *inexpensively* cut the small pieces of wood and veneer used to create the marquetry designs he liked so much.

Eastlake admitted that because machines and technology made it possible for "many articles of ancient luxury" now to be available to the masses, "it would be undesirable, and indeed impossible to reject in manufacture the appliances of modern science."

The "simple" furniture that Eastlake promoted became so closely identified with his book that soon pieces resembling the descriptions and the illustrations in *Hints on Household Taste* became known as "Eastlake furniture." During the time this furniture was in fashion, both furniture factories and individual craft shops faithfully followed Eastlake's "Medieval" or "Gothic" styles.

Interestingly, today we find Eastlake furniture to be anything but simple. It is generally thought to be oversized and cumbersome. In fact, Eastlake is the

one major furniture style that has never been reproduced since the fad faded in the 1890s.

Historically, furniture styles experience a resurgence of popularity approximately one hundred years after their original conception. Though the 1970s saw a few retrospective exhibits, books, and articles about Eastlake, no furniture companies rushed out a new line of Eastlake furniture, and the period pieces saw no marked increase in value.

A PICTURE IS WORTH 1,000 WORDS

Magazines have always shaped public taste, and the influence of lifestyle magazines on the look of the modern home through words and pictures cannot be ignored. Here, for quick reference, are the founding dates of some of the most influential magazines that led to the unequaled popularity of American-made reproduction furniture in the early days.

Godey's Lady Book	1841
Peterson's Magazine	1848
Harper's Magazine	1850
Harper's Weekly	1857
Appleton's Journal	1869
Scribner's	1870
(became *Century* in 1881)	
Ladies' Home Journal	1883
Good Housekeeping	1885
Leslie's Illustrated	
Weekly	1891
House Beautiful	1896
Arts & Decoration	1910
Good Furniture	1910

ARM CHAIR
Seat covered in English

SERVING TABLE

hopeful but modest middle-class family. In the pages of the *Ladies' Home Journal* they saw plans for a new type of home that they could afford—a simple, livable no-frills bungalow.

Great designers of the era—Frank Lloyd Wright, Louis Sullivan, and Gustav Stickley—were also developing "no frills" homes, but one man who is now largely forgotten, Edward Bok, the editor of the *Ladies' Home Journal,* took the affordable, simple home to the masses in a way the elitist craftsmen and architects could not (see page 26).

Loosely based on the English cottage, the bungalow was revolutionary inside and out. Outside, the usual bungalow was a wood shingle or brick one-story home with a front porch covered by a gabled roof.

Inside, numerous changes reflected both the new lifestyle and the new technology. The traditional Victorian "parlor" was replaced by an informal and functional living room. The bedrooms no longer had fireplaces; after all, furnaces and stoves were now being developed to heat the whole house. But the modern kitchen and bath-

> The day of cheap veneer, of jig-saw ornament, of poor imitations of French periods, is happily over.
>
> **—THE HOUSE BEAUTIFUL, 1900**

room had the most innovative changes of all. Needless to say, the response to the bungalow was overwhelming.

This was no place for the oversized Victorian furniture of the preceding decades. These new houses called for a new look. In the distance, the lumber mills were humming, preparing the wood to frame up houses and create new home furnishings.

A Summing Up

Truly remarkable changes occurred in the years between the Civil War days and the last decade of the nineteenth century. Seemingly overnight the masses now had at their fingertips magazines and mail-order catalogs filled with the newest furniture styles. When they strolled downtown they saw these same pieces displayed in the stores. But an even greater event lay ahead.

Capturing the excitement of this growing, prosperous, industrial nation was the greatest, most spectacular exposition ever conceived—the 1893 World's Columbian Exposition.

ARTS AND CRAFTS AND MISSION, 1898–1920

Like Eastlake furniture, Arts and Crafts furniture was created in resistance to the ornate furniture of the Victorian era. And like the Eastlake fashion, the Arts and Crafts style began in England and crossed over to America, where it was interpreted by such fine craftsmen as Elbert Hubbard and Gustav Stickley. The best Arts and Crafts workshops combined painstaking construction methods with the finest materials to create sturdy and well-designed pieces.

Less expensive versions of furniture in the same style, called Mission, were mass-produced by Grand Rapids, Michigan, companies. The Grand Rapids *Furniture Record* distinguished between English Arts and Crafts and American Mission furniture this way: "Mission furniture is really rather a type than a style. Its origin, as the name would imply, is the early Spanish California missions of the Jesuits. An old chair and settee from an ancient mission house, secured by a collector of odd and antique furniture, furnished the inspiration of the style. Nearly contemporaneous with its appearance in this country there developed in Scotland and subsequently in England styles based on somewhat similar lines, called Arts and Crafts."

Today the two terms, "Arts and Crafts" and "Mission," are often interchanged, for the styles look almost identical. Furniture of this type is straight, simple, linear, strong, and mostly devoid of superfluous decoration. Yet though the outward appearance of these pieces may be remarkably similar, there are differences. In the finest craftsmen-made pieces, meticulous de-tailing and internal construction make the difference in quality and, of course, in price.

In 1906 and 1907, Mission furniture was so popular that it reportedly led the sales at the wholesale furniture showrooms. However, according to *History of American Furniture* by N. I. Bienenstock, the editor and publisher of *Furniture World,* some manufacturers nonetheless were totally ignoring Mission furniture while they were busy "resurrecting Colonial, French, and Empire styles." Ultimately those classical, time-tested styles have always held solid while other styles have come and gone.

THE WORK OF L & J.G. STICKLEY

When the purchase of *Good* furniture in plain lines is contemplated the field immediately narrows down to a very few possible sources of supply. Among these "The Work of L. and J. G. Stickley" deserves especial attention for the rare manner in which it blends simple, pleasing design and sturdy usefulness.

L. & J. G. STICKLEY, FAYETTEVILLE, NEW YORK

PART TWO

The Coming Together of Technology and Culture: 1890–1920

4179 Furniture for a Banquet Room in the Manner of the Late Georgian.

A view of the grounds of the Columbian Exposition, held in Chicago in 1893, showing a few of the 27.5 million people who visited it. No wonder it was written that there were "two great classes, those who have attended the Fair and those who have not." At the center is the magnificent Columbia Fountain. The couple (right) is posing before a wooden island with the Electricity and Mines Building in the background.

chapter 3

Things Would Never Be the Same

The Columbian Exposition

Today, the few people who even know of Chicago's 1893 Columbian Exposition think of it as just another "world's fair." But for the 27,529,400 people who attended the Exposition, their view of the world would never be the same. As one writer of the time proclaimed, "After the end of the Exposition all the world may be divided into two great classes, those who have attended the Fair and those who have not."

In the midst of the many changes affecting our end-of-the-twentieth-century lives—fiber optics, laser surgery, fax machines, virtual reality, and the Internet—we have become so used to electronics and machines that it is difficult for us to realize the scope of significant changes brought about by this one exposition at the end of the nineteenth century. Inventions

The Manufacturers and Liberal Arts Building as illustrated in a souvenir book of the Exposition.

we now take for granted and even consider old-fashioned were truly marvels to our ancestors, seeing them there for the first time. My own great-grandfather journeyed from Boston to Chicago to see these wonders, and according to my father, he never stopped talking about them for the rest of his life.

A Majestic Setting for Awesome Exhibits

Chicago was the perfect setting for the exposition. The sweeping fire of some twenty-two years earlier made it possible to construct the necessary buildings in an already established metropolitan area. Instead of timber and brick, the builders used concrete and steel to build innovative, modern structures.

The most awe-inspiring exposition building was the Manufacturers and Liberal Arts Building, also known as the Main Building. Proudly touted as being three times larger than St. Peter's in Rome and four times the size of the Roman Coliseum, it was proclaimed as "one of the wonders of the world." Its Corinthian-style structure was an indication of the coming revival of classical architecture in America. Built of 13 million pounds of steel, 2 million pounds of iron, and 17 million feet of lumber, the $1.7 million Main Building was proclaimed "the most gigantic architectural endeavor of human hands."

Inside, throngs of people strolled along the main corridor of the building, fittingly named

Columbia Avenue. The scene, described by one journalist, "could well be likened to a great thoroughfare in some large metropolis; it might well be termed 'A Road Through the World.'" At every turn exhibits from the leading industrial countries of the world gave visitors a preview of the multitude of new appliances, equipment, and styles, which until now they might have only heard or read about but which soon would be in their very own homes, necessities in their everyday lives.

The sights must have been mind-boggling to nineteenth-century eyes. According to a published list, in the Main Building alone the visitors could leisurely wander among these exhibits:

Chemical and pharmaceutical products, druggists' supplies: Paints, colors, dyes and varnishes: Typewriters, paper, blank-books, stationery: Furniture of interiors, upholstery and artistic decorations: Ceramics and Mosaics, monuments, mausoleums, mantels, undertakers' goods: Art metal work, enamels, etc.: Glass and glassware: Stained glass in

Furniture manufacturers of the turn of the century saw no contradictions in having a mission style chair illustrated in their catalogue on the same page as a Louis XIV reproduction armchair. They were both machine-made pieces inspired by a previous period.

—RICHARD GUY WILSON, THE MACHINE AGE IN AMERICA, 1918–1941

The exterior of the model two-story house, complete with electricity and furnishings provided by the various furniture manufacturers of Rockford, Illinois.

decorations: Carvings in various materials: Gold and silver, plate, etc.: Jewelry and ornaments: Horology, watches, clocks, etc.: Silk and silk fabrics: Fabrics of jute, ramie and other vegetable and mineral fibres: Yarns, woven goods, linen and other vegetable fibres: Woven and felted goods of wool and mixtures of wool: Clothing and costumes: Fur and fur clothing: Laces, embroideries, trimmings, artificial flowers, fans, etc.: Hair work, coiffures and accessories of the toilet: Travelling equipments, valises, trunks, canes and umbrellas: Rubber goods, caoutchouc, gutta-percha, celluloid and zylonite: Toys and fancy articles: Leather and manufacturers of leather: Scales, weights and measures: Materials of war, apparatus for hunting, sporting arms: Lighting apparatus and appliances: Heating and cooking apparatus and appliances: Refrigerators, hollow metal ware; tinware, enameled ware: Wire goods and screens, perforated sheets, lattice work, fencing: Wrought-iron and thin metal exhibits: Vaults, safes, hardware, edged tools, cutlery: Plumbing and sanitary materials: Miscellaneous manufactures not heretofore classed.

EXHIBITIONS AND EXHIBITS

There is no question that the exhibitions and exhibits that brought people and objects together in one place greatly influenced the mind-set of the buying public. In the days before movies and television, choices were made at these shopping extravaganzas. Today, people still visit furniture showrooms in Atlanta, Dallas, San Francisco and of course the grand market held in High Point, North Carolina, or large antiques shows and fairs held across the country where everyone displays their wares. Then, as now, as a result of these exhibits, the most popular styles make it from the showplace to the home.

Here, for quick reference, is a list of the most important exhibits and exhibitions held up to the First World War that influenced the way our ancestors saw the "modern" world as represented by the new products of the day.

CRYSTAL PALACE, LONDON, 1851.

1851	The Crystal Palace Exhibition	London, England
1853	Dublin Exhibition	Dublin, Ireland
1853	World's Fair	New York, United States
1854	Munich Exhibition	Munich, Germany
1857	Manchester Exhibition	Manchester, England
1861	Florence Exhibition	Florence, Italy
1862	International Exhibition	London, England
1867	The Paris Exposition	Paris, France
1873	The Vienna Exposition	Vienna, Austria
1876	The Centennial Exposition	Philadelphia, United States
1877/8	The Metropolitan Museum of Art, Society of Decorative Arts Loan Exhibition	New York, United States
1878	International Exposition	Paris, France
1882	World Exposition	Moscow, Russia
1883	World Exposition	Amsterdam, Netherlands
1885	New Orleans Exposition	New Orleans, United States
1886	New York Bicentennial Loan Exhibition	Albany, United States
1889	George Washington Inauguration Centennial	United States
1893	World's Columbian Exposition	Chicago, United States
1897	World Exposition	Brussels, Belgium
1897	Chicago Arts & Crafts Society	Chicago, United States
1900	World Exposition	Paris, France
1900	Merchants & Manufacturers Exposition	Boston, United States
1901	Pan-American Exposition	Buffalo, United States
1904	Louisiana Furniture Exposition	St. Louis, United States
1915	Panama-Pacific International Exposition	San Francisco, United States

On the Threshold of Tomorrow

Amid all of these wonders, perhaps the most thrilling sight of all to the man on the street was the model two-story house designed by Henry Ives Cobb, one of Chicago's most famous architects, and created by the combined furniture companies of Rockford, Illinois.

The rooms were showstoppers. There was a spacious hall furnished in modern Gothic oak, a French "Colonial" white- and gold-trimmed parlor with "mahogany furniture," and a Romanesque-style dining room with frescoed walls, also furnished in mahogany. But most exciting of all: the house was lighted by electricity. The cost for this model of modern elegance, which was said to be "second to none," exceeded $25,000.

Begin with a Sofa. . . .

The house and its lighting might only have been the stuff dreams were made of for most families, but some of the furniture was within their reach.

> Beginning our quest of a home, we carefully sought out house after house in search of the ideal that we were confident was somewhere to be found.
>
> —ROBERT AND ELIZABETH SHACKLETON, *ADVENTURES IN HOME-MAKING*, 1909

That's why, after touring the house, the visitors stepped into a separate gallery. There the individual furniture pieces on view in the house were available for close-up inspection. And as you might expect, attached to each piece was a card identifying the company that made it—for the viewers' future shopping reference.

While the ladies ooh and aahed over the breathtaking new styles, their husbands most likely wandered over to Machinery Hall, where the amazing new machines that made the house and its furnishings possible were on display. Machinery Hall was second in size and cost only to the Main Building. There, towering over exhibits of "the most marvelous display which mechanical ingenuity and genius has ever gathered to be viewed by man," stood grand, symbolic statues portraying Science, Fire, Water, Air, Earth, Honor, Wealth, and Victory. Below, the machines were divided into the following categories:

Motors and apparatus for the generation and transmission of power, hydraulic and pneumatic apparatus: Fire-engines, apparatus and

The sheer scope and expanse of the exterior of Machinery Hall (opposite), where the new machines that made the furniture were on display, must have been truly overwhelming to the fair goers. Above, the interior of the main corridor of the Hall.

appliances for extinguishing fire: Machine tools, and machines for working metals: Machinery for the manufacture of textile fabrics and clothing: Machines for working wood: Machine and apparatus for typesetting, printing, stamping, embossing and for making books and paper working: Lithography, zinc-ography and color printing: Photomechanical and other mechanical processes of illustrating: Miscellaneous hand tools, machines and apparatus used in various arts: Machines for working stones, clay and other minerals: Machinery used in the preparation of foods, etc.

Seeing so much power housed under one roof had to be truly awe-inspiring, for "the whir of wheels and the clamor of engines is almost deafening, and yet in the midst of all the noise and confusion each machine works hour by hour as if with brains of steel too strong to be dazed or troubled."

The Machines That Would Bring Dreams Alive

Among that multitude of machines that made it possible to turn out affordable furniture for "the

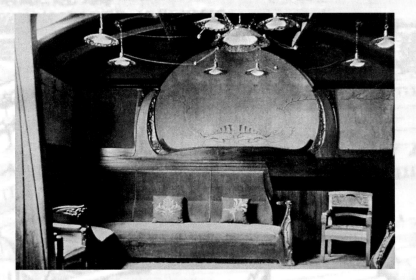

ART NOUVEAU AND OTHER INNOVATIVE STYLES

Looking back on the years immediately preceding World War I in Europe, many exciting and influential movements in design had begun: Cubism, Vorticism, Futurism, Vienna Secessionists, to name a few.

Like Eastlake's furniture of the 1870s and 1880s, these styles involved more than just designs. They embraced broad philosophical views, usually the result of the political unrest in Europe prior to the breakout of the war. Nothing could have been more out of sync with America's more stable mind-set that found comfort and reinforcement of its ideals in nostalgic reproductions of "furniture of the olden times."

Further, on the whole, the styles that evolved from these innovative (some even considered them outrageous) movements did not lend themselves to mass production. The designs required careful handcrafting.

The one European design of the time that had a short-lived fashion in America was Art Nouveau, the hit of the 1900 Paris World Exposition. Still, its flaring lines and high-style ornaments of flowers, insects, and even women with long flowing hair had two things going against it. It was hard to mass-produce and the bold, suggestively sensuous motifs so appealing to the Europeans were hardly to the American taste.

One company more than any other made an attempt at adapting Art Nouveau furniture to the American audience: S. Karpen Brothers of Chicago. By the small number of these American-made pieces that show up these days, the conclusion must be that little was sold.

This European Art Nouveau room (above) was too avant-garde for middle-class America's taste, and the American-made furniture like this sofa by Karpen (left) found few buyers.

millions," as the growing middle-class population was often called at that time, were mills, forges, and looms, weaving and knitting machines. For woodworking there were borers, shapers, trimmers, numerous lines of scroll saws, and finishing machines—all the equipment that made it possible to reduce the cost of furniture by making it easier and faster to carve the wood and slice paper-thin veneers.

Equally important were new steam-drying kilns that enabled companies to cure inexpensive woods so they could be used in mass-produced furniture. Wood costs could be cut further by a machine exhibited by W. W. Grier from Hulton, Pennsylvania, which produced the effect of rosewood, oak, and other "fancy lumber" by ingraining those patterns on pine, bass, and other soft woods "at low expense." All in all, almost any design could now be manufactured quickly, and at a reasonable price.

Only Jacobean-style furniture (above) would be appropriate against the modernized "Medieval" hallway (below, left). Such a setting definitely influenced the tastes of those who returned home and dreamed of having what they had just seen.

A sketch of an English-inspired interior shown at the Columbian Exposition.

Nothing Else Would Do

At the end of their journey through the new lifestyle soon to come, the visitors to the 1893 World's Columbian Exposition had seen the best of both worlds—the world of culture and the world of technology—and they were one.

These impressionable Americans, seeing the furniture and the incredible machines that made it all possible, would now settle for nothing less. Their appetite for the look of "fine things" had been whetted. The new machines put this look within reach of their pocketbooks. The horizon had never looked brighter—especially now with electricity to light the way.

If the late 1890s saw the blossoming forth of the Industrial Revolution, the early 1900s saw the coming of age of the design world. For those who had a stereopticon—and everyone did, for at the turn of the century this was the TV of the day—these interior scene cards would keep the lady of the house abreast of the newest pieces and fashions. (Photos courtesy of the Grand Rapids Public Library, Grand Rapids, Michigan)

Shaping the Public's Taste

Books, magazines, catalogs, and advertisements coached, coaxed, and cajoled the increasingly growing American population into a design-conscious society where style and taste were an outward sign of success. These charming ads (top left and below) for the Karpen Furniture Company, a famous and prolific maker of reproduction furniture, are typical of the era. I selected them from the thousands because the charming insets at the base of each ad harken back to days of yore and touch the nostalgic cord so important at the time.

A t the Paris World Exposition of 1900, seven years after the Columbian Exposition, the main theme of the American pavilion was "America revealing her power and resources." There, a vast mural depicted the Spirit of America lifting her veil. She was flanked on one side by a symbolic figuring representing steam, "the force of the past," and on the other by a figure representing electricity, "the force of the future." That same symbolism was also appropriate to the furniture industry at the dawn of the new century.

The twenty years between 1894 and 1914 were wonderful years in the history of American reproduction furniture. Innovative technology was in place. Natural resources were still plentiful. Craftsmen proudly applied their old-world skills to factory-made pieces. Money was made and spent. The climate of the times made it possible for the romance of bygone years to coexist with the exuberance of the new era.

Arbiters of Taste

The time was also ripe for new mentors of taste to arrive upon the American scene—interior decorators, as they called themselves then. (The title "interior designer" came later.)

In Europe, royal taste had always led the way. In the United States, eighteenth- and early-nineteenth-century craftsmen mostly followed the style and design books written in England and, to some degree, in Europe. Though the craftsmen adapted these foreign concepts to American tastes, these men were furniture makers, not interior decorators or designers.

Sometimes upholsterers and furniture makers gave their clients advice about their wares, but they did not coordinate and arrange entire rooms as a profession. In other words, in those days, there were no "populist" American decorators or arbiters of taste as we know them today to guide the American public in decorating their homes.

Numerous American "household guide" books were written in the 1850s, but these were mostly instructional treatises rather than guides on coordinating fashions and colors. Among the most popular ones were *The Carolina Housewife,* written around mid-century, and the *American Woman's Home,* written in the 1860s by Catherine Beecher and her better-known sister Harriet Beecher Stowe.

A book already often mentioned in these pages, Clarence Cook's 1878 *The House Beautiful,* a collection of "Essays on Beds and Tables, Stools and Candlesticks" that was originally published in *Scribner's Monthly,* had untold influence in home furnishings and broke the ground for the plethora of decorating books that would follow. But it wasn't until the 1890s that the professional interior decorator emerged who would sculpt a room by selecting and properly arranging furniture, upholstery, and accessories. The first proclaimed American interior decorator was a woman, Elsie de Wolfe.

A flamboyant actress with sophisticated taste and skill who worked for wealthy clients, de Wolfe also believed that when the lower class was exposed to fine objects in upper-class surroundings, the influence would trickle down. In her 1913 book *The House in Good Taste,* de Wolfe wrote, "I know of nothing more significant than the awakening of men and women throughout

And where did the decorators get their ideas? By the end of the 19th century the larger furniture-making centers were having exhibits that featured the lines of numerous companies. These pictures are from the Grand Rapids Centennial of 1926. Hepplewhite, Sheraton, Empire, Queen Anne, Chippendale, Jacobean—the classical styles are all represented in fine-quality American-made reproductions. The dining room (above) is Luce Furniture, Cedar Rapids, Iowa; the library (opposite) is Kinney & Levan Co., Cleveland, Ohio (won 2nd prize); and the showroom (below) is Angelo Furniture Co., San Angelo, Texas. (Photos courtesy of Grand Rapids Public Library, Grand Rapids, Michigan)

our country to the desire to improve their houses. Call it what you will—awakening, development, American Renaissance—it is a most startling and promising condition of affairs."

De Wolfe quickly became noted for her decorating of public as well as private places, her cheerful use of color and chintz (she became known as "The Chintz Lady"), and her practical approach to making home life more attractive.

The New, Old Style

Despite all the positive statements that can be made about the trends of this time, there was one shortcoming in the furniture industry—a dearth of new designs. Elsie de Wolfe identified this deficiency when she bemoaned, "We cannot do better than to accept the standards of other times, and adapt them to our uses. We have not succeeded in creating a style adapted to our modern life."

Then she identified a very significant reason why the classical styles were in such favor: "Our life, with its haste, its nervousness, and its preoccupations does not inspire the furniture makers." And we can surely add that the new pace of life made reminders of an earlier time comforting.

period once again became fashionable for a combination of reasons rooted in culture, nostalgia, and technology, new designs took a backseat to the proliferation of the "revised" eighteenth- and early-nineteenth-century styles.

So, as one century drew to a close and another began, the mainstream of taste was for conservative styles. And by the years 1910–19, decorating books and home-decorating magazines instructed the public to fill their homes with copies of earlier style furniture and fabrics, rugs, pictures, and accessories. In short, the decorating books and magazines provided the standard every homemaker aspired to achieve—and that standard imitated the styles of their ancestors.

That Which Had Gone Before

Remember, up until the 1870s there were always new styles coming in fashion. In eighteenth-century England and America there were Queen Anne, Chippendale, and Hepplewhite, followed by Sheraton, Empire, and Victorian in the nineteenth century. In France there were the various Louis designs and the Directoire period. But by the 1880s, when the furniture from an earlier

Traditional Values

To reinforce the importance of traditional values, the same people who were now able to have their own homes and tastefully furnish them fervently believed that the hope for future American generations was rooted in "proper" surroundings.

No one expressed this ideal more strongly than Frank Parsons in his 1916 book *Interior Decoration.* "What, then, can be more important than the house, especially its interior? Is it not here that the child first sees colours, hears sounds, touches textures? Is this not the place where first impressions are received? These impressions should be of the quality one would have the young mind make permanent as standards for future judgment. They will represent what the owner of the house regards as good taste in the gratification of his desires. As the aesthetic sense quickens, the taste for greater subtlety grows, and a changed environment is the result." While optimistic Americans dreamed these uplifting thoughts and aspired to a cultural ideal that would mold future generations and preserve our important heritage, in Europe foreign powers threatened world peace.

War: The Bad and the Good

World War I brought a temporary hiatus to the development of the furniture industry in America. Factories that had been turning out chairs and dressing tables were suddenly turned into manufacturing plants for airplanes, tanks, and gun parts. There was little time to be concerned with luxuries like furniture.

But if the carving and shaping and fret-cutting machines stopped for the war, once peace was declared the usual postwar boom brought unequaled prosperity to both the American population and the furniture companies. The furniture industry began again with renewed energy and verve—and with the advantages of the new technology that had rapidly accelerated during the war years.

Just as technology resulting from the Civil War turned a predominantly cottage industry into the furniture factory industry, so developing technology after World War I catapulted the furniture industry forward. Furniture of every quality,

While the unrest abroad brought a deeper yearning for images traditionally associated with a secure home life and furniture like Nutting's famous reproduction Windsor chairs (above), others who had been captivated by the French style (left and opposite) now sought a more worldly, or sophisticated, look for their homes. (Nutting photo courtesy of Michael Ivankovich)

style, and description could now be churned out to furnish the tract houses that were being constructed at a record rate in every suburban area.

Returning American troops brought with them memories of the sophisticated and elegant French furniture they had seen firsthand. Perhaps a popular song of the era said it best when it asked, "How ya gonna keep them down on the farm after they've seen Paree?" The furniture industry quickly caught on, and by the 1920s the Parisian style became the "civilized" taste.

In an Ever-Changing World, the Comfort of the Old Is Best of All

At the same time, however, American patriotism and the passion for traditional American values was growing ever stronger. The eighteenth- and early-nineteenth-century American furniture styles were more popular than ever. From this postwar climate emerged the great Colonial Revival era in the United States—a stylistic period whose influence eventually proved to be as important as any in our cultural history. During these years Williamsburg was restored to *Colonial* Williamsburg, the American Wing at New York's Metropolitan Museum of Art was opened, and the furniture companies did what the people wanted. They made *reproduction* furniture in every style that Americans had enjoyed in their homes from the seventeenth century straight up to the 1870s, when our story began.

Think about it. Many new furniture styles evolved through the ages—Queen Anne, Hepplewhite, Louis XVI—styles that embraced a whole vocabulary of design elements (like cabriole legs and inlay) and from which every furniture form (chairs, tables, and so on) was fashioned. But as the nineteenth century ended, the coming in of

sweeping new styles slowly died out. The last large innovative furniture *styles* to gain widespread acceptance and to greatly impact American home decor were Eastlake (see page 32), Mission (see page 35), and Golden Oak (see page 29).

From the numerous styles born of the twentieth century only a few *individual pieces* have weathered the tests of time, the winds of change—the Parsons table, Mies van der Rohe's Barcelona chair, the occasional Gilbert Rohde piece designed for the Herman Miller Company, and Charles Eames' chair.

Whatever happened, we must ask ourselves, to the Danish Modern and Mediterranean styles? Even 1990s water beds are made to look like Colonial tester beds, and the entertainment centers that house high-tech TVs, VCRs, and CD players are made to look like Georgian cabinets.

In truth, in the future, when people refer to American twentieth-century furniture, they will not be alluding to one style but rather to the furniture that dominated the entire century, American-made reproduction furniture. Its time has come.

The opening of the American Wing of New York's Metropolitan Museum of Art had a tremendous influence on both the public's interest in their country's decorative arts and their desire to have replicas of such fine pieces. The furniture companies quickly responded.

The Retting Furniture Company ad asks, "May we send you a copy of our booklet, 'How to Know Colonial Furniture'?"
I wish I had a copy, because I genuinely would like to know how the experts of the years 1910–19 and the 1920s
could blatantly mislabel Empire-style furniture "Colonial." No 17th- or 18th-century colonial American home ever had
a mahogany-veneered sofa that even slightly resembled this piece!

Colonial Revival Furniture
Just What Is It?

Antiques dealers and decorators (and this writer) have for a long time been looking for a way to refer to American reproduction furniture other than calling it American reproduction furniture. Of course each style can be called by its specific name, Queen Anne–style, Federal-style, and so on. But a general, all-inclusive name for American reproduction furniture *as a category* is hard to come up with.

Over the years one term has stuck: "Colonial Revival." But what, pray tell, is that?

Today, the term conjures up the furniture bought to outfit the architectural rage of the 1920s, the Colonial Revival home, *as we think of it*—a Federal-style sofa flanked by a couple of Martha Washington–style wing chairs with a Queen Anne–style tea table perched in front of the grouping.

But when reading the typical 1920s or 1930s book on furniture and interior design, you quickly learn that during *that* time, the style of furniture they called Colonial or Colonial Revival was often Empire-style furniture. Everyone knows that American Empire furniture was the furniture made between the Federal and Victorian periods—1820 to 1850. Why would anyone call Empire furniture "Colonial furniture"?

Ask the casual person what furniture styles should be classified as Colonial, assuming you mean that the term should refer to America's seventeenth- and eighteenth-century colonial (pre-Revolutionary or early settlement) days, and they will reply Jacobean, William and Mary, maybe even Pilgrim or Baroque, plus Queen Anne and Chippendale. Empire furniture didn't come along until forty or fifty years after that two-hundred-plus-year period of colonization ended!

By now you realize that Colonial or Colonial Revival can mean anything. In fact, to quote from a book published in 1907, *The Quest of the Colonial,* "the term 'Colonial' is attached to all of the furniture of the early times and the early shapes. It has come to be so generally employed, and is a term in itself so suggestive and so sonorous, that it would be invidious indeed to strive to limit its use with chilly literalness."

After reading that last sentence, who would I be to try to apply a literal interpretation to "Colonial Revival"? But I had to try to explain the broad use (or should I say *misuse*) of the phrase.

As these pages explain, reproduction furniture in the United States really got off the ground circa 1910. Nonetheless, furniture in any variety of styles was coming off furniture factory assembly lines years before then. Faithful reproductions of eighteenth-century furniture were being made by the 1880s.

In Clarence Cook's *The House Beautiful,* a Chippendale corner chair (called an "As-you-like-it Chair") is pictured along with this comment: "The Messrs. Cottier long since found themselves obliged to give up importing furniture from England, as all the pieces that came from

over seas had to be overhauled before they had been many weeks in this country. The chair shown in cut No. 22 is not a modern one, but the Cottiers have used it, or one like it, as a model, and have produced a design that takes the eye of every one who sees it."

What better evidence could there be that copies of European as well as American period antiques had already found a place in the American home?

By 1915, bookcases were filled to overflowing with all manner of books on antique furniture. *The Colonial Furniture of New England* by Irving Whitall Lyons was published in 1891. *The Quest of the Colonial* by Robert and Elizabeth Shackleton was published in 1907. *The Book of Decorative Furniture* by Edwin Foley appeared in 1911 and *Colonial Furniture in America,* Luke Vincent Lookwood's two-volume history, was published in 1913.

Magazines were following suit. *Good Furniture, the Magazine of Good Taste,* published by Dean-Hicks Company of Grand Rapids, Michigan, and filled with advertisements of furniture

From Clarence Cook's The House Beautiful, *the English "As-you-like-it Chair" that the Cottiers were reproducing in New York in the late 1880s.*

Take a close look at this 1915 representation of a "Colonial" room. Other than the two Windsor-style chairs, what piece of furniture therein would anyone in the 1990s call "Colonial"? The writing desk and sofa we would call Empire, or perhaps "Duncan Phyfe" (that misnomer seems never to go away), and the table is clearly a combination of a Sheraton D-end table form fitted with legs that attempt to be Jacobean trumpet-shaped. Such is the confusion we run into when trying to describe much of the reproduction furniture made during the first quarter of the 20th century that has, for years, been labeled "Colonial Revival."

made in America after the eighteenth- and early-nineteenth-century styles, premiered in 1910. Reproductions were so much on everyone's mind that the December 1915 *Arts and Decoration* magazine featured an article on distinguishing good and bad reproductions.

By the years 1910–19 the most popular furniture in America by far was factory-made, assembly-line–produced re-creations of period furniture from Elizabethan times through the Empire era.

So if you take the definition of circa and plop 1910 down after it, you find that the thirty-year span covered therein, 1895–1925, reaches back into the early years of American reproduction furniture on the one side and forward into its glory years on the other. Though reproduction furniture continues to be the staple of America's furniture industry, even in the years of 1990s, the 1910–19 were surely the pivotal years that made the look "The Look." And, the "Colonial Revival" furniture that shaped "The Look" embraced three hundred years of furniture styles, from the 1550s to the 1850s.

HAVING THE BEST MONEY COULD BUY

When Goodyear Tire and Rubber baron Frank Seiberling and his wife, Gertrude, were furnishing Stan Hwyet, their grand, Tudor-style home in Akron, Ohio, in the years 1910–19, they could have bought wonderful period antiques for a song. Instead, they bought expensive, custom-made American reproductions in a variety of styles.

Today, when people seem willing to spend almost any sum on period antiques that speak of taste, longing for quality, and even potential investment, why, we wonder, would the Seiberlings, along with the Reynoldses (American Tobacco money), McFaddins (oil money), and untold numbers of other fabulously wealthy scions choose *reproductions* for their American manor homes? The answer lies in deep-seated pride.

During the early years of the twentieth century the new technology responsible for mass-produced reproductions of "furniture of the olden times" was a source of national pride. Naturally, the newly rich whose money was rolling off the assembly lines of the Industrial Revolution wanted the very finest "new" products on display in their homes.

True, the Rockefellers, Garvins, Fords, and Flints were busy collecting everything from entire towns and villages to pewter mugs and silver porringers, but not everyone had the inclination to spend the time, or acquire the knowl-

Of course R. J. Reynolds and other self-made American millionaires wanted the finest money could buy! And among the best was the newest and most expensive American-made furniture. Machines had made these men wealthy. They respected the new technology and the products made in American factories. This sweeping view of a room in the Reynolds' home, Reynolda House in Winston-Salem, North Carolina, shows the strong English influence and a mixture of furniture styles, some period antiques and some American-made reproductions.

At the McFaddin-Ward house in Beaumont, Texas, the c. 1910 "Sleepy Hollow Chair"(abocve), came from S. Karpen & Brothers' catalog. The great lines and fashionable style of the dining room chairs (right and opposite, bottom) made for Stan Hywet attest to the appeal of reproduction furniture.

edge, necessary to become an antiques collector and connoisseur.

Anyway, some Americans under the spell of European opulence would hardly be satisfied with the comparatively simple lines of eighteenth-century American antiques—even if they were our native crafts. But combine traditional eighteenth-century styles with an updated twentieth-century dressing-up and a touch of English or Continental styling and you have just the right look for their European-influenced homes.

That's what the Seiberlings' New York City decorator, Hugo F. Huber, thought when he commissioned the David Zork Company, a Chicago shop that offered interior decorator services, custom-designed and -made furniture, plus antiques, to create wonderful American-made reproductions for his English Tudor home.

Records show that for the solarium Zork provided two marble-top pier tables, one fall-front lady's desk, a caned armchair, a caned settee, a piecrust tilt-top tea table, a red Chinese Chippendale hanging wall cabinet, two Chippendale armchairs, a pair of ottomans, a Chinese Chippendale armchair and loveseat, a tall case clock, plus a fire screen, book stand, and wastebasket.

Looking at these stylish and superior-quality reproduction pieces today, it is little wonder that the Seiberlings had great reason to take pride in these pieces "Made in the U.S.A."

PART THREE

The Best and the Worst:
The Furniture of
the 1920s

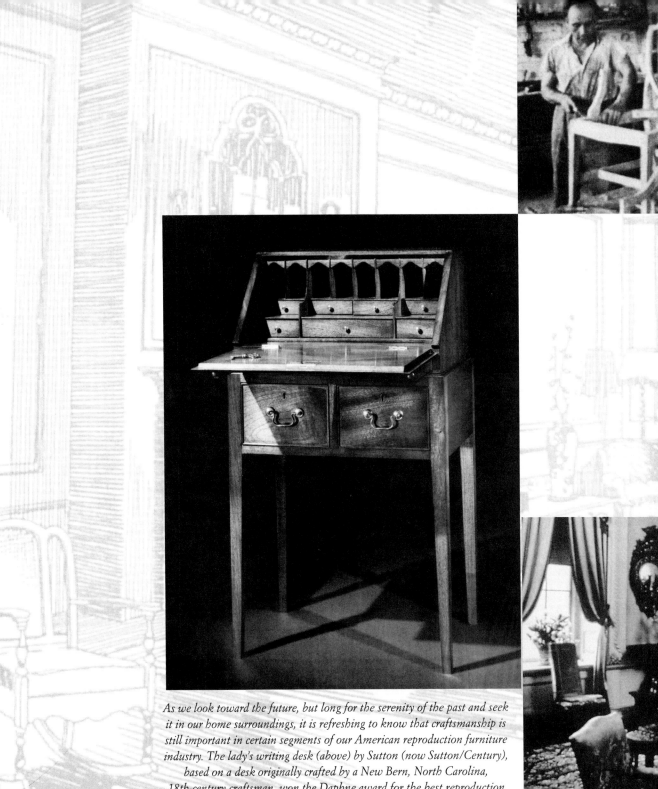

As we look toward the future, but long for the serenity of the past and seek it in our home surroundings, it is refreshing to know that craftsmanship is still important in certain segments of our American reproduction furniture industry. The lady's writing desk (above) by Sutton (now Sutton/Century), based on a desk originally crafted by a New Bern, North Carolina, 18th-century craftsman, won the Daphne award for the best reproduction built in the United States in 1983. (Photo courtesy of Charles Sutton)

The Swan House in Atlanta.
(Photo courtesty of the Atlanta History Center)

chapter 5

Abundance Challenges Taste

Simple, Artistic, Bright, and Attractive

W hat is our modern life?" the *Practical Book of Interior Decoration* asked in 1919.

The authors answered their rhetorical question: "It is undeniable that there is in our present existence . . . an element which is hectic, freakish, anarchistic and unwholesome." According to them, "modern" styles were the outgrowth of this chaos.

Yet, they admitted, times were changing and Americans were now poised for "a movement which awakens and 'gives them to think.'" For those who preferred the old but were also forward-looking, the authors recommended "a method of decoration well adapted to modest houses, cottages and some apartments, which is simple and at the same time artistic, bright and attractive." In other words, reproduction furniture.

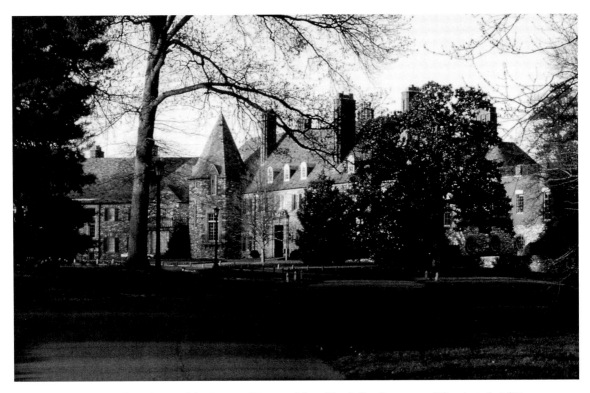

Graylyn, the magnificent home of the Grays in Winston-Salem, North Carolina, exemplifies the palatial European-influenced houses that were built from New York to California during the years 1910–19, the 1920s, and occasionally even the very early 1930s. (Photo by Walter Smalling)

The Call of Suburbia

Just as middle-class Americans a generation earlier had dreamed of owning a "bungalow," the young people of the 1920s dreamed of a "rose-hedged home" in suburbia.

In these postwar years, the world was shrinking faster than ever before. New technology spurred on by the war was explosive. Chrome, plastic, metal tubing, aluminum, plywood, and all other sorts of new materials were invading every avenue of life. In the factories, faster and faster machines were turning out more and more products cheaper than anyone could have envisioned even twenty-five years earlier.

Houses in any variety of styles were springing up along newly paved, electric-lighted streets with bucolic, sonorous names like Oxford Lane, Elm Street, Park Drive, and Virginia Avenue. The designs for these homes were based on magazine and newspaper blueprint plans bearing such names as English Country, Dutch Colonial, Spanish Hacienda, French Provincial.

While the fabulously wealthy who were making fortunes in steel and rubber, finance and real estate, were building French Chateau– or English Tudor–style palatial homes having seven, twelve, or twenty or more bedrooms and countless baths, the large and ever-growing middle class was happy to settle for a three-bedroom, one-and-a-half-bath home. In short, it was an idyllic time that blended the best of the old with the best of the new.

Only antiques or antique-styled furniture was suitable to furnish the homes that had their origins in earlier centuries and foreign countries. The English Tudor style was so popular that the home furnishing store W. & J. Sloan bought the entire interior of the English artist William Hogarth's eighteenth-century London home, and another English house was purchased by wealthy industrialist Richard Craine, who donated half of it to the Art Institute of Chicago and installed the other half in his Ipswich, Massachusetts, country home. Meanwhile the interior decorators of the day mixed period antiques and reproductions with seventeenth- and eighteenth-century tapestries and untold miles of imported fabrics to complete the luxurious, romantic look of these mini-estates.

And for the middle class? Great quantities of mass-produced English Tudor–style furniture for more modest suburban homes were churned out in every price range and quality by the whirring machines at Baker Furniture Company, Grand Rapids Upholstering Company, Phoenix Chair Company, Washington Parlor Furniture Company, and Valentine Seaver Company, to mention just a few.

Do It Yourself

This enormous new market for home furnishings created a field day for home and lifestyle magazines. Monthly issues grew thicker and more elegant. *House Beautiful* put out *The House Beautiful Building Annual* and *The House Beautiful Furnishing Annual.* Now, even without the services of a personal interior decorator, the wife could confidently decorate her home from the wainscoting to the floor covering, for every aspect of her "house beautiful" was discussed and illustrated in their pages. Only her pocketbook held her back.

The Best of the Best

Upscale magazines made no bones about it. The only acceptable reproductions had to be "faithful" copies of the original pieces. The 1925 *House Beautiful Furnishing Annual* advised its readers: "The secret in selecting good furniture lies in the choice of pieces each of a form strictly true to the type it represents, not a hybrid product showing

In this interior view of a much more modest home, a convex mirror similar to the grander one shown in the Swan House (page 67) is hung above a nice reproduction Chippendale-style slant-front desk.

in itself the elements of several different types of period design; and secondly, in the use of combined period styles, in the judicious selection and association of types of design which are closely related through some dominant common interest, either chronological, such as Adam, Sheraton, Chippendale, and Hepplewhite, or racial, such as Spanish and Italian."

The companies creating forms "strictly true to the type it represents" were proud of their accomplishments. "No imitator

There is no war between art and industry but that, for their mutual benefit and self-preservation, they must help each other. By such means a great and noble national art may become the hereditary birthright of every American citizen.

—WILLIAM LAUREL HARRIS, "THE UNWRITTEN HISTORY OF MACHINERY AND ART IN THE UNITED STATES," *GOOD FURNITURE*, OCTOBER 1916

could achieve the fine proportions, the color, nor the sculptured quality of carving," proclaimed one company about its reproduction Duncan Phyfe table. "His [Phyfe's] personality was infused into every part of his work and no detail, however insignificant, was overlooked, as is evidenced in this exquisitely proportioned card table."

Echoing the familiar phrase "there aren't enough antiques to go around," the Company of Master Craftsmen in 1927 advertised, "Fortunately, or unfortu-

Say "museum" and you immediately think "antique" and "18th century."
As we approach the 21st century and our interest in the early 20th century heightens, house museums that capture that time are attracting more attention. The McFaddin-Ward House in Beaumont, Texas, is a treasure trove of American-made reproduction furniture. The footstool (below and right) is labeled John Miller & Co., a prominent decorator who advertised reproductions in Good Furniture *in the years 1910–19, and the gateleg table (left), though unlabeled, is typical of this immensely popular style and form of the early 1900s. (Photos by Chip Henderson)*

At Swan House in Atlanta the chintz slipcovers on the sofa manage to give a lived-in look to an otherwise grand and opulent home of the sort that inspired the middle class to copy, on a smaller scale, the look of the mansions. (Photo courtesy of the Atlanta History Center)

nately, modern machinery cannot make real antiques. Yet, without consideration of expense, we find that the majority of our customers prefer a fine reproduction of a beautiful piece to a poor or excessively restored original. But to make a reproduction with the charm of the antique is no easy task; no average organization and no ordinary factory could accomplish it. The Company of Master Craftsmen was organized to meet this situation."

How did they meet it? According to the advertisement:

First: To this Company was brought a group of well-trained woodworkers, able designers, adept cabinetmakers, and skillful finishers. . . .

Secondly: A spacious, well-lighted factory was built in Flushing, Long Island, and was equipped with the most modern devices to assist in a comparatively rapid production of highly perfected product.

Thirdly: All reproductions are taken from original pieces, which are transported to the fac-

While a handful of companies like Wallace Nutting targeted the highly knowledgeable and most discriminating buyers (left), the majority of the furniture manufacturers aimed their ads toward a broader segment of the market (below). These companies also usually added a little touch to a basic design—something not too expensive (they wanted to keep the price down), but an eye-catcher, so to speak. In the instance of this otherwise plain Sheraton-style sideboard, that touch was a swag hung over a patera and bellflower on each drawer. This would be fine except that these motifs are not part of the Sheraton design vocabulary, as explained further in chapter 6. (Nutting photo courtesy of Skinner Auction Gallery)

A · CONTRIBUTION · TO · THE · MODEST · HOME

By THE TORONTO FURNITURE COMPANY

Made in Mahogany and Walnut and finished dull.

In light of the growing mechanization of the factories, many companies made an effort to stress craftsmanship in their advertisements.

tory whenever possible, and are made available for reference as the work progresses. In addition to these great advantages, the workmen have also the advisory aid of the best-known students and critics of antique furniture—European and American.

Yet another quality furniture company, Albert Grosfeld, maker of "reproductions, for contemporary use, which combine the traditional skill and art of European craftsmanship with the requirements of our trade," told in their catalog how, for upholstered furniture, "the frames are designed by us, assembled, finished and upholstered in our New York factory. The carvings are all done by hand. All frames unless otherwise specified are finished in patinated walnut. Frames may be ordered in special shades of walnut, without extra charge, or in antique crackled-painted finishes at slight extra cost."

The time in which we live is one of eclecticism. Our artists and designers, with the vast and diverse art treasures of the past to inspire and serve them, do their work more in a spirit of interpreting accepted historic forms than in a spirit of invention. Our architects and designers are not trying to originate a distinctly new and American *style*. In their most productive moods they are rather adapters of old forms to new conditions, and in new combinations.

—*Good Furniture*, February 1916

The Other Choices

If all the companies had had these high standards we would have no poorer-quality reproduction furniture. But then, neither would the less wealthy "millions" have been able to afford the look they so admired.

This market purchased lower-priced pieces that can only be described as loosely adapted, scaled-down copies made from cheaper materials. The November 1927 issue of *Antiques: A Magazine for Collectors and Others Who Find Interest in Times Past & in the Articles of Daily Use & Adornment Devised by the Forefathers* spoke harshly of this broad audience which it called "hordes of folk whose intelligence quota is, and always will be, below the average. What these people want, and will want, is not something that, in so far as its limitation of price go, is really good and suitable, but something which satisfies their moronic notions of elegance, or which appeals to their sentiment by virtue of some familiar association."

Looking back on the 1920s, I, like the writer in *Antiques,* wish that only faithful reproductions had been made, but they weren't. We can't change that. But what we must be sure of is that *we* know enough to be able to *distinguish* the best from among the infinite amount of reproduction furniture that was made "circa 1910."

It is as true in the 1990s as it was in the 1880s, the 1900s, and the 1920s that *quality* is what sets a piece of furniture apart, and quality is based on the successful combination of style, materials, and construction.

Suter's finely crafted corner cupboard is in the tradition of yesterday's heirlooms but suitable to today's lifestyle. (Photo courtesy of Suter's)

'ill Be Proud to Have This Italian Renaissance Dining Suite in Your Home

e and well constructed, but priced at a bargain, this high quality burl room furniture will stand the test of time, both in point of service and Honor Bilt," a convincing guarantee of satisfactory service; the Italian esign is recognized as a standard and lasting style in fine furniture. The ship and superior grade materials are apparent at a glance have figured walnut upright matched veneers in fronts and tops. Burl shaped overlay decorations. Tops, fronts and solid ends, five-ply; backy ttoms, three-ply. Drawer bottoms are mahogany veneered; drawers and finished inside; boxed-in drawer construction. All parts not veneered are hed to match. Famous Duco finish, either American (dark) or French ave metal glides; other pieces have casters.

Height, 43 inches; removable tray for silver. CHINA CABINET—Top, eight, 66 inches. EXTENSION TABLE—Top, 45x54 inches; height, 30 lock. Three 12-inch leaves. WOOD BACK SIDE CHAIR—Seat, 18x16 above seat, 23 inches. WOOD BACK HOST CHAIR—Seat, 21x17 inches seat, 24½ inches. UPHOLSTERED BACK SIDE CHAIR—Seat, 19x17 above seat, 22 inches. UPHOLSTERED BACK HOST CHAIR—Seat, height, above seat, 25 inches. (All upholstered chairs come in taupe ather or tapestry.) SERVING TABLE (not illustrated)—Top, 19x36 36 inches.
pped from factory in INDIANA. Any of above furnished separately.

I D 2359½ Buffet	Shpg. Wt. Lbs.	American Walnut (Dark) Finish	French Walnut (Light) Finish
Top, 22x60 inches	225	$43.65	$43.75
Top, 22x66 inches	250	47.75	47.85
Top, 22x72 inches	275	51.85	51.95
China Cabinet	175	34.65	34.75
Extension Table	225	36.75	36.85
Serving Table (two-door cupboard)	100	19.65	19.75

	Shpg. Wt. Lbs.	Tapestry	Blue Leather	Velour	Tapestry	Blue Leather	Velour
Wood Back Side Chair	15	$7.95	$8.00	$8.25	$8.05	$8.10	$8.35
Wood Back Host Chair	18	10.45	10.50	10.75	10.55	10.60	10.85
Upholstered Back Side Chair	17	10.60	10.65	10.90	10.70	10.75	11.00
Upholstered Back Host Chair	20	13.10	13.15	13.40	13.20	13.25	13.50

While some reproduction companies like Albert Grosfeld strove to keep such traditions as hand carving alive (right), far more companies were slapping precut veneered decorations onto cheap frames stained to look like more expensive woods (above). Unfortunately and, I think, unfairly, those are the companies that have given all reproduction furniture a poor reputation, regardless of its quality.

Chapter 6 is your guide to recognizing quality American-made reproduction furniture. These pieces will be the antiques of the next generation.

Eleanor Roosevelt and Val-Kill Furniture

It seems hard to believe that students of the American furniture industry could forget about Eleanor Roosevelt's role in the creation of American-made reproduction furniture, yet few people know of Val-Kill furniture. Mrs. Roosevelt lovingly wrote about her involvement with this handcrafted furniture in her 1949 biography *This I Remember*.

The year was 1924. Franklin Roosevelt was immersed in his rising political career and the Roosevelts had little time or privacy. Their refuge

In the late1920s and early 1930s Eleanor Roosevelt supported Val-Kill, a handcrafted reproduction furniture line created in upstate New York and sold through a Madison Avenue showroom. (Photo courtesy of National Park Service, Roosevelt-Vanderbilt National Historic Sites, Hyde Park, New York)

was Val-Kill Cottage, a stone cottage that Roosevelt himself helped design and build beside Val-Kill brook in Hyde Park, New York. But, as Mrs. Roosevelt later wrote, "The cottage was not an end in itself. It was the place in which Nancy Cook and Marion Dickerman lived and from which Miss Cook directed a furniture factory."

Nancy Cook longed to reproduce copies of early American furniture, but not, Mrs. Roosevelt stressed, "worm-eaten antiques." Using as prototype pieces from the Metropolitan Museum of Art, the Hartford Museum, and private collections, Cook developed a line of fine-quality reproductions suitable to furnish upscale Colonial Revival homes that were springing up across the country during this time. Seeing that this was an opportunity to involve underutilized farm workers in a new industry that could flourish in the countryside, the Roosevelts lent their full support to the idea. It was a natural match. Everything about the project appealed to the social-conscious Roosevelts: it would train young people for meaningful employment; it would keep them close to home; and it would foster a love for the old and the historic.

Eleanor Roosevelt gave more than just her time and influence to Val-Kill furniture. She invested earnings from her speaking engagements and writings, as well as some of her own inheritance in the project. Using this funding and local workers to turn out Chippendale-style chests and Queen Anne–style chairs, pewter pieces and woven textile, Mrs. Roosevelt, Nancy Cook, Marion Dickerman, and Caroline O'Day, another friend, kept the factory going through the early years of the Depression. Then, in 1936, like so many other noble enterprises that fell victim to the increasingly worsening economic times, their experiment ended and the shop closed.

"I never made any money," Mrs. Roosevelt wrote. Rather, she admitted, "I was probably one of the best customers the shop had, because I bought various pieces of furniture as wedding presents and as gifts for other occasions." Eventually the factory building was turned into apartments, and finally it became Mrs. Roosevelt's year-round home after Hyde Park was given to the National Park Service.

The site where Val-Kill furniture was made still stands. While the factory itself is gone, many pieces of Val-Kill furniture are still present at the Eleanor Roosevelt National Historic Site and at the famed Little White House in Warm Springs, Georgia, where President Roosevelt died. For more information, see the directory.

These two catalog pages from Val-Kill furniture show the range of styles produced by Eleanor Roosevelt's noble project. The more formal scene (opposite, top) features pieces that were created based on English styles: a late-17th-century Welsh dresser; an early-18th-century Queen lowboy; and a dining table and chairs loosely adapted from the 19th-century pieces. The less formal scene (below) depicts the popular early American or Colonial style. (Photo courtesty of National Park Service, Roosevelt-Vanderbilt National Historic Sites, Hyde Park, New York)

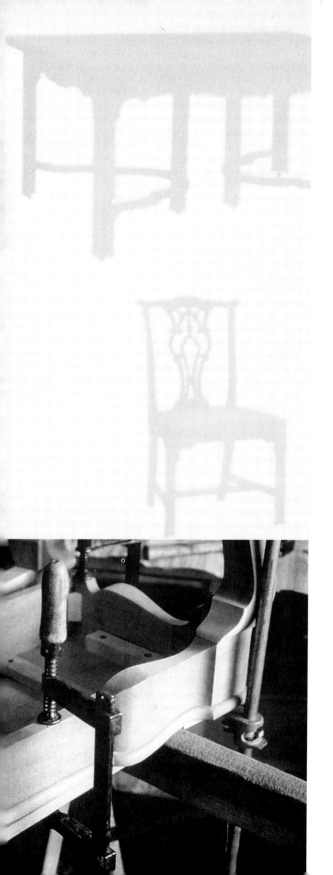

chapter 6

Behind the Making of the Styles

Wallace Nutting, the Congregational minister turned furniture maker and antiques guru of the early twentieth century, must have had a crystal ball when writing the preface to the *Supreme Edition* of his company's furniture catalog in 1930.

"Persons furnishing homes are not in the habit of doing so to enhance their fortunes," he wrote. "But it is a bald fact that the value of my furniture increases faster than most good investments. And while this is going on the furniture is a continual source of satisfaction, a pride, a comfort and a distinction. I am getting elderly. Shrewd business men have told me that pieces bearing my name will soon be coveted by collectors. The thought did not originate with me. Think it over."

Those lucky people whose grandparents did think it over and bought Nutting reproductions are finding these pieces both durable and attractive *and* coveted by a whole new breed of

Who says craftsmanship is dead? Even among the large furniture manufacturing companies a love for wood and fine furniture lives on. These pictures from Kindel show the painstaking steps that go into creating fine museum-quality antiques for the 1990s home. There is a real place for reproduction furniture, because after all, there can be only one home for the original period antique but many people wish to have the constant pleasure of its beauty and design in their own homes. (Photos courtesy of Kindel Furniture Company)

collectors. Why? Because Nutting's furniture was largely handmade and of excellent quality.

Nutting's reproductions were expensive. In the days when the typical good-quality, mass-manufactured slant-front Chippendale-style desk sold for $100 to $150, a comparable Nutting piece cost about $300. But the investment paid off. Today, that Nutting reproduction desk can be expected to sell in the $2,000–$3,000 range. That's almost as much as some *period* eighteenth-century slant-front desks. That's as much as some brand-new, mass-manufactured Chippendale reproduction desks.

But not all of our grandparents could either afford or wanted Nutting's fine pieces. Most of them, in fact, bought the $100 desk. Our job now is to be able to identify the $100 desk and the $300 desk, whether we are weeding through the pieces our ancestors bought or shopping for old reproduction furniture to furnish our homes today. After all, these pieces are still around, though they are getting harder to find. For, as Rick Barentine, director of the Furniture

> **People of education like stylish and solid furniture. Such furniture gives a background to life and will last hundreds of years and grow in value every year.**
>
> **—WALLACE NUTTING, 1930**

Factories Marketing Association of the South in High Point, North Carolina, said, "[M]ore of these pieces are in our mind's memory banks from our grandparents' homes than are in the museums today."

Value or Sentiment

This means that many people are eager to buy the finer, old reproductions while they still are accessible and affordable. Then there are those faced with deciding which of their family's pieces to hold on to and which to dispose of.

In that second group, some will decide it does not matter one bit how good or bad a piece is—they will always want to keep it for sentimental reasons. Others will assess each piece on the basis of appearance and quality and then decide if they wish to have it in their own homes. There is room for both ways of thinking because ultimately the objects we choose to have around us are meaningful only to us. What is important is that information about this vast, but largely overlooked,

When Wallace Nutting bragged in the 1930s that pieces bearing his name would be coveted by collectors, he was right on target. The handcrafted block-front chest of drawers (left) as pictured in the old catalog sold originally for $130. Today, Michael Ivankovich, who has made a lifetime study of Nutting's works, says its value is in the $2,000 to $4,000 range. (For another example, see photograph bottom right on page xix.) There aren't many of these pieces around today because Nutting made only a limited number of them. In addition to the satisfaction of seeing the prices for fine early American-made reproduction furniture increase, there is the added pleasure that comes from uncovering the maker of some of the pieces.

The past was everywhere you looked in the first quarter of the 20th century. The joint Grand Rapids Furniture ad for all the Grand Rapids companies featured craftsmen of old creating a 17th-century Jacobean chair (below), while the Elgin A. Simonds Company of New York took the potential furniture buyer through the periods in their "Heirs of all the Ages" ads (right and bottom) showing our forefathers (idealized, of course) giving their approval to reproductions based on the

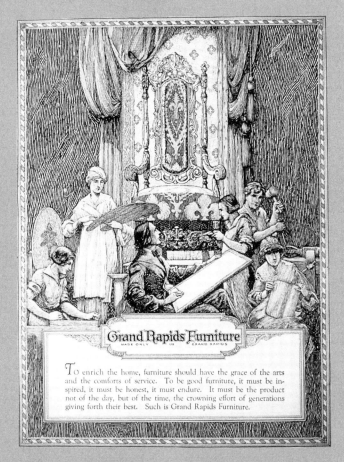

furniture styles of their times. Why not? After all, as the Hampton Shops proclaimed in their ad (opposite) in the March 1919 Vogue, "The flickering firelight from the hospitable open hearth with its architecturally conceived overmantel in some noble paneled room of olden times, not only falls on the dusky oaken furniture surrounding it, but may flash a message of cheer to the home-maker of the later days." Of course this later-day homemaker could find just the right

THE PERIOD PAGEANT

The drama of the great furniture periods is over, but the Epilogue plays on—and neither actors nor scenery have lost all their glamour

table and chairs in "The Traditions of our Forefathers at the Hampton Shops!" An old copy of an ad for Homefurnishing Arts, *a 1920s publication, added a truly dramatic tone to reproduction furniture, complete with nostalgic drawings (right) that told the world:* "The drama of the great furniture periods is over, the Epilogue plays on—and neither actors nor scenery have lost all their glamour."

Where did these ideas originate? No illustration

shows the source of inspiration better than the pictures taken from the March 1925 feature article, "American Furniture Design" *by Ralph G. Erskin, in* International Studio. *About the chest (top left) he wrote,* "An American chest of the first period, made of oak and pine with squash ball turnings and pegged joints, possesses inspiration for modern office furniture." *Then he showed just such a desk (below), described as* "A desk for the modern office, illustrating the application of conventional details in design and construction, taken from the chest of oak and pine shown above."

period of home furnishings be available for those who want to know about it.

When accessing the quality of reproduction furniture the two most important factors to be considered are:

- quality of construction
- quality of design

Construction

This book is not intended to show how to distinguish period antiques from later reproductions. Any number of books cover that subject, including my own *Guide to Buying and Collecting Early American Furniture.* Rather, this book is written to explain more about the history of early American-made reproduction furniture. But it is helpful to know that generally speaking, once truly advanced, electric-powered machines were developed and put in place around the turn of the century, reproduction furniture was turned out by four different processes.

HANDMADE FURNITURE

First is the craftsman who, working alone or with just a few others, continues to make furniture "the old-fashioned way." These devoted craftsmen still cut dovetails by hand and chisel out mortise and tenon joints. They carve backsplats and hand-rub the finish until the surface is gleaming and beautiful. By the late nineteenth century these craftsmen were quickly disappearing, and today the breed is almost extinct when compared to the number who were once working.

At the turn of the century nearly every town of any size had such craftsmen whom everyone knew about by word of mouth. Unfortunately,

Ever since Colonial times, small crossroads towns and country byways have been home to fine craftsmen who have found the materials, as well as the solitude, they need to create fine furniture. In 1914 Ralph Erskine's fine handcrafted furniture, made in Tryon, North Carolina, a small Southwestern mountain town, was sold on Madison Avenue in New York City and advertised nationally.

few of these skilled craftsmen ever signed their pieces. Nonetheless the *quality* of their work is universally recognized.

Today, though such craftsmen can still be found, seldom do they advertise nationally. They may put out a catalog or brochure and keep a small storefront, but even then you may have to make an appointment to see their pieces. Like their counterparts of an earlier time, their pieces are commissioned and expensive. Though the greatest cluster of these craftsmen seems to be in the New England area, with a little digging chances are you can find one working near your home. Among the best known of these craftsmen are Christopher Bretschneider, Donald Dunlap, David LeFort, and Louis Irion.

In the directory I have compiled the names of many such craftsmen, as well as workshops that fall into the next category.

BENCH-MADE AND CRAFT-SHOP FURNITURE

More frequently found these days are craftsmen who, while maintaining the integrity of the original design and taking the time to hand-carve decorative ornaments and hand-rub the finish, nonetheless use modern equipment to facilitate making the pieces. Their operations may employ ten, twenty, or more people, but seldom are these businesses large enough to take massive orders from furniture stores or chains.

Like the makers of handmade furniture, these craftsmen usually show their wares only in relatively small showrooms. It was from such an outfit that I bought my very first furniture as a bride in 1962.

Mr. Howardton (I never heard anyone call him by any other name) had a street-front store in Clarksville, a Virginia hamlet close to the North Carolina border. Clients came from far and wide to custom-order simple-styled but well-constructed and -designed corner cupboards, beds, dressing tables, and chairs.

Displayed alongside Mr. Howardton's reproduction pieces, which were made in the workshop out back, were some of the true period antique pieces that he copied. A few savvy customers talked him out of these pieces. "You can have it. I've got a copy," he would say. But by and large, his customers wanted pieces made by Mr. Howardton himself. These days, when I drive through Clarksville, even though

To celebrate the tradition of bench-made reproduction furniture, the Moser Company commissioned this wonderful oil portrait, framed in wood, depicting Charles Moser in his workshop using tools that date back to the turn of the century.

Howardton's Antiques, as his business was called, is no longer in existence, I remember the trips I made there many years ago. I am still proud that at age twenty-one, I commissioned Mr. Howardton to make the Queen Anne–style dressing table and stool that I continue to enjoy to this day.

Just an hour's drive from Clarksville is Lynchburg, Virginia, the home of Moser Furniture Company. Back in the 1940s and early 1950s, Luther O. Moser, Sr., employed as many as thirty-five craftsmen to build their reproductions. But times change and today Charles Moser, Luther's son, is the only one making furniture. He's seventy-five. The rest of the staff, including David Moser, Luther's grandson, operate a retail

ing the quality of construction of reproduction furniture whether it was made seventy-five years ago or last week. In the Hepplewhite-style chair (inset A) shows how arm posts are joined into the seat rail and then glued and securely screwed to provide maximum strength. Inset B illustrates how carefully shaped wooden hinges are joined to the Pembroke table's case by a round wooden peg. This mechanism provides secure support when the leaves are up and is out of sight when the leaves are down.

"When I see some of the modern production techniques and compare them to the old methods, what I don't see is craftsmanship," said my friend Joe Rees. "What I see is assembly-line production—staples, glue, and particle board plus spray-on finishes shot out of hoses with high-pressure air-feed nozzle guns drying under ultraviolet light curing and ready to ship out the door." Joe knows what he's talking about. He's a crackerjack textile engineer who loves antiques. Joe's mostly right. But some companies are still involved in doing things "the old-fashioned way." Here, from Suter's Handcrafted Furniture catalog, are clear illustrations of the steps they take to ensure that their reproduction pieces will become treasured family heirlooms.

Study these illustrations because they show you where you should look and what you should look for when assess-

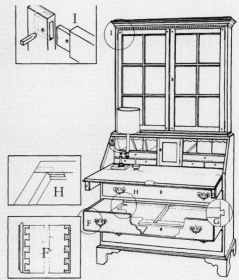

To ensure stability and yet be able to be easily taken down when moving, in traditional tall post beds, the side and end rails are cross-bolted (inset C).

Case pieces—chests, cupboard, secretaries, and desks—have numerous stress points (above). For greatest strength, dovetails are used to join drawer fronts and backs to the sides (inset F) and to join the rails that separate the drawers (G) to the case of the piece. Because wood expands and contracts as the humidity changes, mortise and tenon joints (inset H) are used to secure the drawer side runners to the front and back rails. Where doors are present on a piece, pegging gives them added strength. The inset illustration (I) shows how the parts are first mortised and tenoned and then secured by inserting a peg that has been dipped in glue into a hole that goes through the mortise and tenon joint.

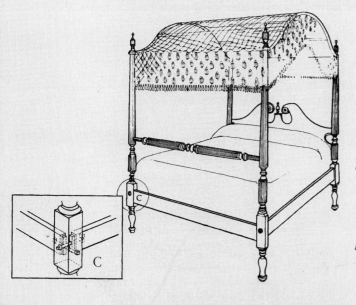

marine business. As David says, "The folks around here already have my father's and grand-father's furniture. Now we're selling boats to their kids."

At Moser's, equipment used seventy years ago is still being used today. And the furniture is being made the same way. Charles' description of how these small operations work is the best one I've heard. "We rough the material out with the tools and then we take it to the bench and hand-craft it."

If you keep going west from Lynchburg over to Harrisonburg, Virginia, you will come upon Suter's Handcrafted Furniture Collection, another family-owned furniture company that continues a tradition begun by Daniel Suter more than 150 years ago.

Suter's has some twenty-five or so craftsmen who turn out furniture for their two showrooms, one in Harrisonburg and another in Richmond. Carol Suter, who runs the business today, explains that though more power tools may be used, drawers are still dovetailed to provide the strongest joint possible and doors are still mortise and tenon–joined and pegged for a sturdy fit. Each pane of glass is individually hand-set in the corner cupboards and every piece is hand-rubbed to a satin-smooth finish.

In other words, the craftsmen at Suter's are taking the same steps craftsmen all across the country were taking back in the 1910s when they created the durable, faithful, and beautifully crafted pieces we take so much pride in today.

It is by chance that the three shops with which I am so familiar are all in Virginia. In truth, they serve as a microcosm for what was happening in Maine, Iowa, Florida, and every state where there were craftsmen, lumber, and customers in the early days of the twentieth century. Today, such

Cost-consciousness has always been a part of marketing. The best deal has always been getting the look you want combined with good quality and at a reasonable price. Good American-made reproductions make all that possible.

workshops as Wright Table Company in North Carolina, Donald Dunlap in New Hampshire, and Eldred Wheeler in Massachusetts are among those keeping the tradition alive.

MACHINE PLUS HAND

When it comes to true mass production, as we have seen, as early as the later nineteenth century, large companies continued to incorporate a few labor-intensive steps in order to produce a fine product that combined modern mechanization with yesterday's skills. These were the companies that were selling their wares to the big furniture

Luck was with me when I visited Becky Dykstra in California many years ago
. . . if not with her! She had two circa 1920 Kittinger chairs—one in as-new condition (top left), and one in as-is condition. From these pictures you can see the
excellent construction techniques that have long made the Kittinger name outstanding among furniture manufacturers—strong dowels, pegs, and corner
joints. If you're wondering how the one became "as is," unfortunately it was
half-dropped, half-thrown off a moving truck. Even steel will bend under those
conditions. As an interesting postscript, at right is a very similar chair made
during the same time by another fine-quality company, Baker.

stores. These were the companies that could afford to market and advertise their name and look in hopes that customers would walk into a store and say, "I'd like to see your Berkey and Gay (or Century Furniture Company, or Elgin Simonds, or whomever) pieces."

Only a few of the early companies still exist today. Baker Furniture Company, which celebrated its hundredth birthday in 1991, comes immediately to mind, as do other such familiar names as John Widdicomb, Kindel, Howard Miller Clock Company, Hekman, and Sligh.

Today, many well-known companies maintain the integrity of the original style while incorporating the most modern techniques, including laser cutters and lacquering. Several in this group produce furniture lines for museums and restorations. Yet because cost is always a consideration, various companies turn out a wide assortment of pieces ranging in price from the tens of thousands of dollars for an outstanding breakfront or secretary to a few hundred dollars for an occasional table or hanging shelf. In other words, quality can vary greatly within this third group.

Among the currently working companies that combine, in varying degrees, mechanization and hand processes are Baker, Kindel, Sutton/Century, Hickory Chair, and the Masco group—Henredon and Drexel. These companies also use the finest materials. There are no fake drawer bottoms and backs used here.

MACHINE-MADE REPRODUCTIONS

Finally, there are the cost-conscious manufacturers that must meet the tremendous demand of the public for beds and chairs, tables and desks, at a price that everyone can afford. This group

> Cheap furniture is turned out through the elimination of quality— "watering the glue," as the workmen call it—and where quality is eliminated certain and rapid dilapidation is sure to occur.
>
> —MAUD ANN AND HENRY BLACKMAN SELL, *GOOD TASTE IN HOME FURNISHING*, 1914

No matter how good a buy a piece of furniture seems to be, when inexpensive materials have been used, this short-coming eventually shows up, as when this large hunk of veneer split off when the glue loosened.

*Good design is at the heart of distinguishing quality in
reproduction furniture. Even a cursory glance at the
Chippendale-style chair (above) tells you the proportions are all off. The seat and legs are too broad for the
short back. As far as the amusing remark about the
"exceptional" antique reproduction that "Mr. P———"
had never seen anything like, I assure you that no
17th-century cavalier had ever saw anything like the
reproduction china cabinet (top right) loosely based on
Jacobean concepts, and that when I saw the turn-of-the-
century Queen Anne–style potty chair complete with
modern toilet seat (right), I, too, was aghast!*

has been the largest segment of the furniture industry by far since the turn of the century. Construction techniques and the materials they use determine the quality of their lines. At an earlier time such companies as Estey, Holland, Phoenix Chair, and Ward fell into this group of manufacturers. Today the names are Bassett, Broyhill, Singer and Stanley, American Drew, and Thomasville. Then, as now, the lines such companies produce usually include look-alikes made of less costly materials as well as adaptive designs that keep alive the *spirit* of the epoch, if not the actual furniture styles of the period.

Design, the Ultimate Test

No matter how well constructed a piece of furniture is, if it is poorly designed, it is an eyesore. Unfortunately, when the demand for reproduction furniture outpaced the supply and the public, uneducated in styles, gobbled up whatever was offered, many furniture designers discarded all standards of beauty and form. Stumpy pieces, wobbly pieces, out-and-out ugly pieces took their places next to beautifully designed and crafted furniture. Sadly, too often only the sophisticated, educated eye could tell the difference.

(Photo courtesy of Michael Ivankovich)

WALLACE NUTTING

"Whatever happened to the antique reproductions of renowned furniture maker Wallace Nutting?" begins a press release from Berea College, tucked away in the beautiful rolling foothills of Kentucky's Cumberland Mountain range.

Kentucky? As in "My Old Kentucky Home"? Why Nutting, that Massachusetts native and longtime Maine resident who exemplified the born-and-bred Yankee if ever there was one?

I read further. "Probably the largest collection of his efforts is displayed at Berea College." It seems Nutting had taken an interest in this liberal arts college, which began to provide quality education and sound values to students from the southern Appalachian region, and in 1900 delivered the college's commencement address. During his forty-year association with the school, Nutting helped develop Berea's Woodcraft Program as a center for fine furniture making. Nutting even trained two Berea instructors in his methods at his Framingham, Massachusetts, factory.

Upon his death in 1941, Nutting bequeathed his furniture, factory, and blueprints to the college. The factory was sold and in 1945 almost two hundred pieces of handcrafted Nutting furniture were shipped to Berea, where they remain for study and continue to serve as exemplary models for making fine reproduction furniture.

For more information, see the directory.

A faithful reproduction of an 18th-century Queen Anne highboy made by the Baker Company in the first part of the century.

Bowing to the Process

As Rick Barentine explained, the furniture manufacturing companies simply bowed to the manufacturing process. If a Queen Anne–style back could be turned out more cheaply than a Hepplewhite-style back, they made the Queen Anne–style backs. But if the Hepplewhite-style leg was quicker and cheaper, then *that* is what they attached to the Queen Anne–style back.

The Choices: Faithful, Adaptive, or Hodgepodge Combination

Times haven't changed. The best reproductions of the classical furniture styles, be it Jacobean or Hepplewhite, Chippendale or French Empire, are those that *faithfully* adhere to the lines, dimensions, decorations, and spirit of the original styles, whether they were bold and robust as was

Charles D. Thomson addressed this issue in the April 1915 issue of *Good Furniture* with this anecdote: "A critical buyer was recently shown such a piece [a poorly designed reproduction] by a proud salesman, who said: 'And what do you think of *this,* Mr. P——, as an antique reproduction?' 'Well,' replied the former, 'it certainly seems exceptional, and in fact, I think I can assure you that I never before saw anything like it!' "

Chippendale furniture, or dainty and restrained as was Hepplewhite.

Next best, design-wise, are the reproduction pieces that were changed slightly to better blend into the look and scale of the twentieth century but still maintained the integrity of the earlier period. These "adaptive" pieces, as they are called, were turned out by the majority of the top-line furniture companies.

Least desirable of all are those furniture styles that combined various components from numerous styles into a new look. The problem arises because each of the classical styles has a consistent, unified look all its own. When you begin taking the design of, say, a delicately shaped leg here, a bold and strong backsplat there, and add an ornament from heaven knows where, there is no continuity in design. Aesthetically it just does not work, no matter how well constructed or what excellent materials were used in the piece itself.

The Best Always Will Be the Best

When it comes right down to it, Wallace Nutting's words ring as true today as they did nearly three quarters of a century ago. What could be better than to surround yourself with furniture that is at the same time a "continual source of satisfaction, a pride, a comfort and a distinction" and a good investment. Knowing how to assess *quality* is the first step to that end.

This Queen Anne–style lady's dressing table (opposite) is a figment of a 20th-century furniture designer's imagination in its lines, wood choice, and the presence of the attached mirror. Mirrors were separate pieces of furniture in the 18th century, and this one is definitely Victorian in its shape and ornamentation. In other words, this is a fanciful hodgepodge of a piece.

Just remember what quality is. In furniture, whether period or reproduction, it is the combination of

- line and balance
- the suitability and execution of decorative details and embellishments
- the use of fine materials
- solid construction
- finish

Happy antiquing!

A good adaptive copy of a Queen Anne secretary-bookcase made in the 1920s by Kittinger. The scale of this piece is in keeping with 20th-century homes, and the cornice is not truly of period styling, but the use of burl walnut and its general appearance resemble that of similar pieces of the period.

chapter 7

Furniture Styles: Period Pieces and Later Reproductions

Styles: Old and New, Good and Bad

The Furniture Library in High Point, North Carolina, is a wonderful source of trade catalogs, magazines, and archival material on the American furniture industry, as, of course, are the Public Museum of Grand Rapids, the Grand Rapids Public Library, and the Winterthur Library. But High Point is so close to my home in Raleigh that I can drive there in less than two hours.

Over the years I became good friends with the library's founder, N. I. Beinenstock, affectionately known as Sandy and to whose memory this book is dedicated, and the curator, Carl Vuncannon. It was only natural that one day, while watching the library visitors come and go, I asked Carl what most people are hoping to find when they come here.

The ad tells you this is a reproduction. "But in what style," you may wonder? Distinguishing the styles of reproduction furniture is often complicated by the mixing of several styles in the creation of one piece, as many of the illustrations in this chapter will show. The settee in this circa 1916 ad is for a Jacobean-style piece based on an English 17th-century design.

The interior decorator, or the dealer whose patrons are connoisseurs of fine furniture, are invited to avail themselves of the remarkable scope for selection afforded by the John Miller assortment of reproductions.

Many periods and many countries have been drawn upon for models in this fine assortment of

Reproductions of Historic Furniture

A. H. NOTMAN & COMPANY, Selling Agents
Salesrooms: 121-127 W. 27th St.
New York City

JOHN MILLER & COMPANY
517-520 East 17th Street
New York City

Many reproduction furniture makers took the basic form and style of a piece from an earlier time and simply adapted the original design to the modern home by scaling down its size and toning down the ornamentation of the period to better suit the 20th-century eye.

Exceptional Suites in Every Style
for the Dining Room, Living Room, Bed Room and Hall

These suites completely cover the different styles so much in vogue at the present time at prices which will interest you.

Blue Prints of any part of the line will gladly be mailed at your request

Grand Rapids Chair Company
Grand Rapids, Michigan

"Styles," he replied without hesitating. "People come in and say, 'I've been told I should buy Queen Anne furniture. Do you have some books that can show me what Queen Anne pieces really look like?'"

Carl's answer not only told me what people need to know, it helped me decide how to organize this chapter, for some furniture books are arranged by form—chairs, tables, desks, and so on—rather than style.

Here, then, are brief descriptions of the various styles of furniture most often reproduced by American furniture companies during the 1880–1930 era, and of course continuing on to today. Accompanying each written description are illustrations, both of period pieces and of various reproductions of the styles.

Some of the reproductions illustrated are "faithful" copies, as they were called at that time, whereas other reproductions pictured are *adaptions* of the original period style as they were designed for "modern" lifestyles.

Also pictured are reproductions that, for lack of a better word, are bastardized pieces which combine any number of elements from different styles all in one piece. An example of such a piece is a secretary-bookcase that brings together a Chippendale pediment with Hepplewhite inlaid doors, a Jacobean paneled lower section, and Sheraton reeded feet! It is, as they say, neither fish nor fowl. No student of period antique furniture would ever give such a piece a second glance, yet many such pieces are thought to date from the 1780s or 1790s, rather than the years 1910–19 and the 1920s.

Just remember, when you see such pieces, common sense dictates that they can be no older than the youngest style element. In other words, the very earliest time that secretary could date from would be the Sheraton era, or around 1810 or 1815. And the designers of Sheraton furniture never incorporated Chippendale, Jacobean, and Hepplewhite elements in their designs. Beyond the exterior design of the framework, of course, the telltale interior construction would positively date the piece as an early-twentieth-century secretary.

A. J. Johnson & Sons Furniture Company wrote about this circa 1915 sideboard:
"The carvings and ornament are different, the hardware is different—each piece is a work of art in design. . . ."
"The piece itself certainly is different," the devotee of faithful reproductions wants to reply. This piece combines a basic Sheraton design with quasi-Adamesque ornamentation and a Louis XVI embellishment at the center of the backboard that is totally out of place because sideboards were never part of French dining room furniture. Whenever you see old manufactured pieces having several combined elements taken from different classical furniture styles, you can be sure you are looking at a fanciful 20th-century reproduction.

Historically, there is no such piece of furniture as a Queen Anne sideboard. Hepplewhite is credited with originating the sideboard form almost fifty years after the Queen Anne period had begun to fade and had given way to the new fashion, Chippendale furniture. Yet here is a sideboard with cabriole legs that definitely define the piece as a "Queen Anne–style sideboard." Note the attached mirror at the back. Mirrors were precious commodities during the 18th century, especially the early years of the century when Queen Anne reigned. Even if there had been such a furniture form as a Queen Anne sideboard, it would not have had a mirror attached to it!

Then there is yet another category of American-made reproduction furniture: those pieces copied after an early style but in a form that did not exist until the later nineteenth or twentieth centuries. The piece that springs instantly to mind is the coffee table.

There were no coffee tables in the eighteenth or nineteenth centuries. They had tea tables back then, but they were totally different from the modern coffee table. Tea tables were tall and intended to be used in front of a tall-backed chair or sofa from which the hostess served tea. Coffee tables, on the other hand, are low resting (not serving) places for cocktail glasses, coffee cups, and of course the ubiquitous coffee-table book. The concept of the low-slung coffee table did not appear until the 1920s, which means that even those "antique-styled" coffee tables cannot be a century or two old.

Study this section on styles very carefully. These days, much is being written about furniture construction, yet relatively little has been written about the giveaway styling and design of much reproduction furniture that immediately labels it as what it was made to be—reproduction furniture.

When compared to the later classical period styles, little period Jacobean furniture has survived. There are two commonsense reasons for that. First, the Jacobean era was during the 17th century. That was a long, long time ago. It only follows that war, natural disasters, and just plain cleaning out and leaving behind lead to the destruction of much furniture. Second, not as much furniture was made during the 17th century and only a small amount of that would have been attractive enough and of sufficient quality to survive down through the years. Here are two pieces of period Jacobean furniture.

Above is an extremely rare 17th-century cupboard. Only a quick glance at this monumental piece and you know the demand for pieces of such form is going to be minimal in the 20th century. On the other hand, the very late period Jacobean American highboy (left), made just as the Queen Anne style was coming in, is much more suitable to modern living. Twentieth-century furniture designers took the look and ornaments used during the era, while the ad agencies played up the romantic "pilgrim" angle. The result was the production of untold quantities of Jacobean-style furniture. Jacobean-style reproduction pieces are identifiable by these characteristics.

(Photos courtesy of the Museum of Early Southern Decorative Arts, Winston-Salem, North Carolina; Craig and Tarlton)

Jacobean Style

General characteristics	Furniture forms	Ornaments
solid and heavy	chests and chests of drawers	geometric panels and designs
dark woods	arm- and side chairs	bold turnings
highly carved	tables, beds, desks	trumpet shapes
square, rectangular shapes	all sorts of "modern" forms including cabinets, low tables, Victrolas, etc.	ball and bun feet
teardrop brasses		spindles, scrolls, and spirals
cane seats		

The finest-quality reproduction Jacobean-style furniture captured the robust spirit of the era by using bold turnings and heavy, solid oak in the re-creations of forms true to the lifestyle of the 17th century. Pictured is Wallace Nutting's Jacobean-style chest, distinguished by the use of black ornaments in keeping with the period.

Jacobean Period Furniture, 1558–1702

The earliest furniture style used by the American furniture industry as a basis for reproductions was the furniture of Queen Elizabeth I's reign—1558 to 1603—the Renaissance era. Historically, this was the beginning of domestic furniture as we know it today. Practically no furniture survives from the preceding Medieval era, though Renaissance literature, inventories, pictures and art, plus actual pieces, build a body of evidence of what life was really like during this time.

But it was during the ensuing hundred years, including the reigns of James I and II, Charles I and II, William and Mary, and the eleven years from 1649 to 1660 when Oliver Cromwell was the Protector of England, that domestic furniture came into its own.

Taken as a whole, from 1558 to 1702, when Queen Anne ascended the throne, furniture changed little. It was large and heavy, based on straight lines, decorated with carved panels or spiral turned parts, mostly made of oak, and very often wretchedly uncomfortable. (The spiral motif—a technical and artistic accomplish-

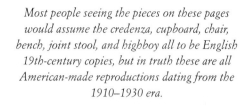

Most people seeing the pieces on these pages would assume the credenza, cupboard, chair, bench, joint stool, and highboy all to be English 19th-century copies, but in truth these are all American-made reproductions dating from the 1910–1930 era.

ment during the period—would be the style's downfall when it was later copied by modern furniture companies.)

Over these many years several furniture forms evolved—cupboards, joint stools, gateleg and trestle tables, and eventually the first upholstered seating furniture. Furniture of this time is variously referred to as Tudor, Renaissance, Baroque, Carolean, William and Mary, but most people can call up a vivid image of the furniture of this time when they hear the term "Jacobean."

JACOBEAN-STYLE FURNITURE

In the hands of the American furniture designers approximately two centuries later, Jacobean furniture took on a whole new look. Granted the square, boxy lines and decorative motifs were retained, but suddenly

this oversized furniture took on a lighter air. It had to. American homes were not open, drafty, monumental-in-scale English or Scottish stone castles. These were homes with divided rooms—living rooms, bedrooms, dining rooms, and eventually music rooms and sun porches (the forerunners of family rooms and dens).

New pieces that the denizens of the sixteenth and seventeenth centuries had never heard of appeared in the furniture stores labeled "Jacobean." Cabinets with glass doors, something the Elizabethan courtier never saw, and slant-front writing desks (another form unknown in 1600) having drawers decorated with spindle turnings and teardrop pulls were made. All in all, many more *adaptations* of Jacobean furniture were produced than "faithful" reproductions for the simple reason that the original style was too oversized for the modern home. As one decorator of the time advised, "Too much emphasis cannot be laid on the importance of a proper room arrangement and decorations, as the Jacobean style in particular must have a harmonious architectural treatment to be made a pleasing furnishing. Articles of later periods more readily adapt themselves to our usual type of room interior, but the heavy oaken furniture of the Jacobean type should have a proper background of wall paneling, as well as room proportions drawn on a big scale. Crowding large, bulky Jacobean pieces into small, dainty rooms reflects very poor judgment."

Unfortunately, for the most part many of these Jacobean adaptations were among the worst-designed and cheapest-constructed pieces made by American furniture companies. The authors of *Modern American Period Furniture*

It takes the exceptional interior to accommodate the look of the Jacobean era (opposite, top), but the manufacturers of the day tried to show how it could be done. (below and opposite, bottom)

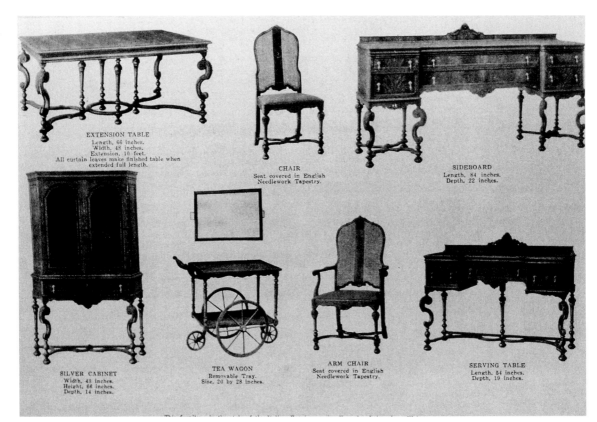

EXTENSION TABLE
Length, 66 inches.
Width, 48 inches.
Extension, 10 feet.
All curtain leaves make finished table when extended full length.

CHAIR
Seat covered in English Needlework Tapestry.

SIDEBOARD
Length, 84 inches.
Depth, 22 inches.

SILVER CABINET
Width, 43 inches.
Height, 66 inches.
Depth, 14 inches.

TEA WAGON
Removable Tray.
Size, 20 by 28 inches.

ARM CHAIR
Seat covered in English Needlework Tapestry.

SERVING TABLE
Length, 54 inches.
Depth, 19 inches.

It should be kept in mind that while the elements of the different period styles of yesteryear are themselves static, the American adaptations are not. There are two reasons for this. One is, that while all the period styles are in permanent demand, the whims of popular fancy year by year register preference for first this period, then that, each of which may be said to be in vogue, for the time being. A second reason is that adaptation, while following along well-defined tendencies in the different styles, gives play to some originality on the part of the modern designer, so that each may bear some touch of individuality. Thus it is that there is a constant and wholesome development in American adaptations, promising much for the future of furniture design.

—BEN H. DEAN AND WALTER J. PETERSON, *MODERN AMERICAN PERIOD FURNITURE*

Scaled-down and totally new forms were created to give the 1900s bungalow house a Jacobean-style interior look.

(that title should give you a chuckle) wrote in 1917, "Recently the Jacobean [style] enjoyed a revival of interest. During this period [the 1900s and the years 1910–19] a great mass of cheap, unartistic furniture flooded the market under the guise of Jacobean because of the presence of a twisted treatment somewhere in the design. Indeed, it appeared that any woodworking plant, possessed of a turning machine, felt itself competent to produce Jacobean furniture. . . . Such developments are unfortunate for the cause of good furniture. Cheap, unprincipled designs, masquerading under the name of a period style,

dull the good taste of the public on whom they are imposed."

The authors blamed the spiral motif of the style for such bad treatment by the companies. The new machines could whip out turned legs, spindles, and stretchers in nothing flat. And so these "twisted" members were used indiscriminately and any pieces with a spiral motif were christened "Jacobean."

More Jacobean-styled dining room furniture was made than any other sort. Sideboards and glass-doored china cabinets, both forms unknown during the period, and massive tables

Spindles were all that was needed to give any piece a Jacobean-style look. These pieces are of decent quality, material, and construction, but the design misses the scope and heft of the Jacobean period.

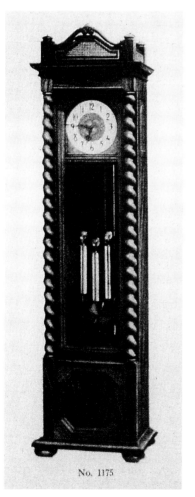

The Jacobean-style Victrola (below) was an essential piece in the music room of a comfortable upper-middle-class home—the equivalent of our den or family room today—while the clock (left), with bold spiral turnings on the case and a caned inset at the pediment, was often the focal point of the foyer.

No. 1175

No. X. Victrola Cabinet.

Scores of dining room furniture was made in the Jacobean style and buffets of the sort shown at right are seen everywhere today, as are circa 1920 bedroom pieces (below) that really defy any one style but are loosely called Jacobean because of the trumpet-shaped legs.

Least desirable of all are those poorly designed and veneered Jacobean-style pieces that were inexpensively made to begin with and are no better today.

II   V   IV   I   VIII   VI   III   VII

An assortment of Jacobean-style ladies' writing desks as the 20th-century furniture designer wished they had looked in the 17th century.

perched on turned legs were showy, inexpensive pieces. Running a close second were ladies' writing desks like the ones pictured above. True, some writing desks were made during the later Jacobean period, but like the piece about which "Mr. P—" commented, "I think I can assure you that I never before saw anything like it!," so no seventeenth-century court lady ever saw a desk that looked like these.

A typical Jacobean-style radio; note the turned legs.

Queen Anne Period Furniture, 1702–1760

The Queen Anne style was developed in England during the reign of Queen Anne (1702–1714) and with slight modifications remained popular throughout the reigns of her two successors, George I and George II, or until about 1760. During this time in England, dramatic changes took place in living standards, quite noticeably in middle-class homes. No longer were everyday comforts demanded only by the rich. A furniture style suitable for homes, rather than palaces, was needed. And so whole new industry began when cabinetmakers who filled this need flourished.

Queen Anne furniture is characteristically much lighter and more graceful than the preceding Jacobean and William and Mary styles. In England walnut was mostly used in the construction of these pieces, but mahogany was used as well.

The most notable and easily identifiable characteristic of the Queen Anne style is its curved shape, a line found in the beautiful but simple cabriole legs that are distinctive of the period, in the rounded seats, in the chair backs that were often "spooned out" to allow for more comfortable sitting postures and had curved crest rails, in the arms that curved and flared outward, in the arched pediments that topped chests and cabinets, and in the scalloped aprons that gave style and grace wherever they were added.

The wood surfaces were quite often plain—note the solid fiddle, urn, or vase-shaped splats of Queen Anne chairs. Sometimes, though, a carved cockleshell motif was used on the knees of the

These two period Queen Anne pieces are featured to show how a surface can be left clean and simple, as with the tea table (below), or be highly carved, as with the lowboy or dressing table (above), though each piece is based on the same basic design. Carving added the cost of a highly skilled craftsman in the 18th century, so only the very wealthiest customer could afford such expensive embellishments. Once machines that imitated hand work were available, the fancier, more elegant look could be had at a fraction of the cost of a hand-carved piece, and only slightly more than the cost of a plain-surfaced piece. (Tea table photo courtesy of Craig and Tarlton; dressing table photo courtesy of the Museum of Art, Rhode Island School of Design, Pendleton Collection)

The shape of the leg is one of quickest and surest ways to identify a furniture style. Compare this Queen Anne–period highboy (above) to the Jacobean one with trumpet-shaped legs on page 99 and you immediately see what a difference the legs can make to the overall grace and appearance of a piece. The graceful, curving cabriole leg and the vase-shaped backsplat, another curvaceous line (seen in the chairs at left), are the distinctive motifs of the Queen Anne style. (Photo courtesy of Craig and Tarlton)

QUEEN ANNE STYLE

General characteristics	*Furniture forms*	*Ornaments*
refined, graceful	high- and lowboys	shaped aprons
mahogany or walnut	arm- and side chairs	shells and scrolls
curved, sensuous lines	tables, beds, desks	simple pad feet or ball-and-claw feet most usually used
vase-shaped backs	all sorts of "modern" forms including china cabinets, low tables, Victrolas, tea carts, and sideboards	
cabriole legs		

SERVING TABLE
Top, 17 by 46 inches.

ARM CHAIR
Slip Seat.

EXTENSION TABLE
Top, 54 inches diameter.

CHAIR
Slip Seat.

SILVER CABINET
Height, 72 inches.
Width, 40 inches.

SIDEBOARD
Top, 25 by 72 inches.

CHINA CABINET
Height, 72 inches.
Width, 40 inches.

Queen Anne–style pieces individually shown (above) and arranged in a room setting (opposite).

cabriole legs, or added to an apron or drawer, or to the crest rail of chairs.

Stretchers were only occasionally used during the Queen Anne period, and then mostly on earlier pieces. Queen Anne feet are predominantly slipper feet—sometimes padded, sometimes not—although ball-and-claw type, web-shaped, and Spanish scroll feet were also used.

On the case pieces of furniture during the period—chests and tables with drawers, for there were *no such pieces as period Queen Anne sideboards and armoires*—bail handles and either plain or slightly chased escutcheons were used.

Other Queen Anne pieces made during the period include high and low chests; side, arm-, and wing chairs; settees; dining tables of the drop-

At the Voigt House Victorian Museum in Grand Rapids, Michigan, an 1870s Victorian mirror is flanked by a William and Mary reproduction chair by Berkey and Gay on one side and a Queen Anne reproduction chair by the Dexter Company on the other. (Photo courtesy of the Voigt House)

Pictured below is a rare and important period Queen Anne secretary-bookcase. (Photo courtesy of Craig and Tarlton.) In startling contrast at right is a bastardized 1915 adaptation of the form—a rather dumpy lacquered and floral-decorated fall-front desk of the secrétaire à battant style.

In addition to the "modern" concept of the Queen Anne sideboard, another out-of-period form often found is the record player resembling the Queen Anne cabriole shape.

Few period japanned or chinoiserie-decorated pieces have survived the years of constant dusting, the cracking and pealing that come from ever-changing temperatures and humidity, as well as the fading from bright sunlight. But countless numbers of early-20th-century lacquer reproductions do survive.

Its legs are too skinny. Its back has lost its sensuous curves. But to the American furniture designer, this scaled-down version of a Queen Anne–style chair (above) was just fine. To the connoisseur, it has lost its character.

A line of Queen Anne adaptations produced by Berkey and Gay in the years 1910–19. Notice the presence of the sideboard and cabinet. This picture was taken from a boxed series of pamphlets designed, according to a letter signed W. J. Wallace (obviously an officer of Berkey and Gay), to provide solutions to the problem of creating "harmonious furnishings" for the modern home.

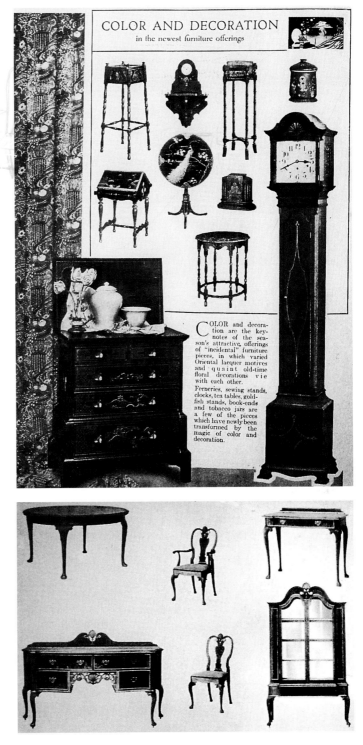

COLOR AND DECORATION
in the newest furniture offerings

COLOR and decoration are the keynotes of the season's attractive offerings of "incidental" furniture pieces, in which varied Oriental lacquer motives and quaint old-time floral decorations vie with each other. Ferneries, sewing stands, clocks, tea tables, goldfish stands, book-ends and tobacco jars are a few of the pieces which have newly been transformed by the magic of color and decoration.

The Queen Anne lines were perfect models for smaller-scaled writing desks. Here are two good-quality Queen Anne–style reproductions from among the many designs of writing desks made during the early 20th century. Note, however, that the one by Aulesbrook and Jones (right) is a far looser interpretation of the style and materials of the period than the one by H. C. Valentine & Co. (below).

No. 918¾ Desk Chiffonier
Top, 22 x 40.
Desk closed has same appearance as
Drawer Front.
Made in Mahogany also.

Of all the early furniture forms, the one piece that has had the greatest difficulty surviving the ages—at least up until the first part of the 19th century—is the bed. Modern mattresses and changing heating systems and sleeping patterns make more contemporary bedding definitely preferable to most people. Here is an example of how 20th-century furniture designers adapted the feel of the Queen Anne curved line to a modern bedroom suite.

leaf variety; occasional tables including card and tea tables; writing desks; and serving tables.

QUEEN ANNE–STYLE FURNITURE

What reproduction furniture maker could resist copying these beautiful forms 150 and 200 years later? Even today, the Queen Anne style remains the most popular style ever created. As a result, unlike the much maligned Jacobean style, early on, many reproductions of the Queen Anne style were faithful, carefully measured, and skillfully crafted pieces.

During the Queen Anne period, a very small percentage of English pieces were lacquered in the labor-intensive process known as chinoiserie or japanning. Only a handful of period American chinoiserie pieces have been documented, but the appeal of this elegant and showy style was irresistible. During the years 1910–19 and the 1920s, black-, red-, and green-lacquered Queen Anne pieces decorated with various intricately detailed Oriental scenes became all the rage. Some of the best of these later-made pieces combine several aspects of fine craftsmanship—from basic furniture design to construction techniques to the artistic decoration.

December magazines always featured small furniture items. In this Ovington's ad you see an assortment of Queen Anne–style 20th-century pieces that were to be bought as delightful accent pieces.

Extreme liberties also were taken in the scale of the chairs. Period Queen Anne chairs were fully fleshed out and beautifully proportioned. But as furniture designers created smaller-scaled furniture for less ample dining areas, Queen Anne chairs grew all around skinnier and slimmer. The end result was a wobbly, bandy-legged chair (see page 111).

Another Queen Anne piece singled out by modern furniture designers for adaptive design was the secretary-bookcase. In truth, few of these pieces were made during the period. But scores of them were mass-produced in the early twentieth century. Like adaptive Queen Anne chairs, these modern variations are often too tall, too skinny, too skimpy to be aesthetically correct or historically accurate.

Just as the spiral motif used in Jacobean furniture gave the furniture companies an easily mass-produced part, so the beautiful, shapely Queen Anne leg was an unbeatable form guaranteed to find a following even when used on fanciful tea wagons and sideboards. But as John Andrews writes in his *Price Guide to Victorian, Edwardian, and 1920s Furniture,* "Oh well, why not?"

Chippendale Period Furniture, 1750–1790

Chippendale is the name given to period furniture of the latter half of the eighteenth century made in the style of Thomas Chippendale, the first English cabinetmaker to have his name attached to a particular style. Chippendale was as much a businessman as an artist, inviting prospective customers to tea in his salon where, of course, his finest furniture was displayed.

Soon his workshop became *the* meeting spot for London's most fashionable and artistic personalities. In 1754, Chippendale's *The Gentleman and Cabinet Maker's Directory* was pub-

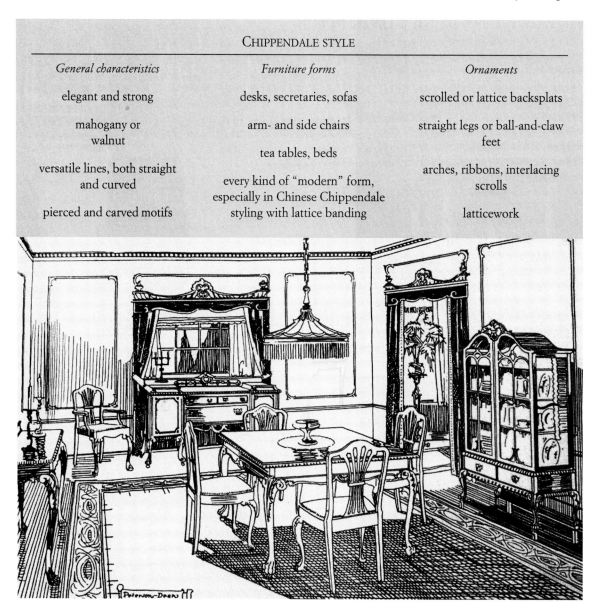

CHIPPENDALE STYLE		
General characteristics	*Furniture forms*	*Ornaments*
elegant and strong	desks, secretaries, sofas	scrolled or lattice backsplats
mahogany or walnut	arm- and side chairs	straight legs or ball-and-claw feet
	tea tables, beds	
versatile lines, both straight and curved	every kind of "modern" form, especially in Chinese Chippendale styling with lattice banding	arches, ribbons, interlacing scrolls
pierced and carved motifs		latticework

Elegant 18th-century Chippendale furniture is timeless. Not only was the furniture of the period stunning in appearance, but much more of it was made for the growing well-to-do merchants and bankers and professional classes in both England and America. The period secretary-bookcase and comfortable wing chair are perfect examples of the expanded forms and great stylishness that evolved during the second half of the 18th century. (Photos courtesy of Craig and Tarlton)

lished in London. As other craftsmen copied these styles, "Chippendale" parlor and dining room pieces became essential for the stylishly furnished home.

Chippendale and his followers used mahogany almost exclusively to build structurally sound furniture. A strong wood, mahogany lent itself well to the elaborate carving that was signature to this style. Though English in origin, Chippendale furniture was equally popular in the American colonies, thereby creating an air of unparalleled elegance and stateliness in home furnishings on both sides of the Atlantic. Thanks to this combined popularity and durability, large quantities of period Chippendale pieces are still around.

Stylistically, both flowing curves and straight lines were used in Chippendale furniture, as were adapted Rococo, Gothic, and Oriental elements. For example, while some Chippendale chairs

Study these two different lines of Berkey and Gay Chippendale-style furniture carefully. The line shown at the top could easily be called Queen Anne. Note the cabriole legs and modified vase-shaped backsplats of the chairs. But the tacking on of the broken-arch pediment is a strong Chippendale motif. Look back at the illustration of the period Chippendale secretary-bookcase on page 115. This combination of curved and straight lines is often found in Chippendale and Chippendale-style furniture. The other Berkey and Gay line (below) has definite Chippendale influence and is more easily identified as Chippendale style.

Few people would take a chair like the 20th-century furniture designer's Chippendale-style sketch (right) seriously. Though it has all the earmarks of the Chippendale period—a typical pierced and scrolled backsplat and straight legs with Chinese Chippendale carving—the results are more humorous than attractive. A much better, more traditional rendering of an 18th-century Chippendale chair is

the faithful reproduction shown in the middle, at left. Still, though, were it placed side by side with the period Chippendale chair (middle right), a comparison of the materials, construction, patina, and wear would instantly prove the 125-year age difference between the two. (Photos courtesy of Craig and Tarlton)

were made with carved cabriole legs (a carryover from the Queen Anne period) combined with the new style of ball-and-claw feet, others were made with straight, sometimes carved or reeded, legs with or without supporting stretchers.

Chippendale chair-back designs were generally straight, supported by straight uprights, and topped with curved or serpentine crest rails. Chair seats were square and tended to taper toward the back. When arms were present, whether straight or curved, they usually were joined to the uprights at an angle.

A fine 18th-century chair incorporating cabriole legs, with strong Chippendale ball-and-claw feet and a masterfully carved pierced backsplat. (Photo courtesty of Craig and Tarlton)

The ever-irresistible Chinese Chippendale style was immensely popular among the more sophisticated reproduction furniture companies, but unfortunately it was also quickly adopted by other companies as well.

But the ornately pierced and carved chair back (see bottom photograph, page 117) was the most innovative and distinctive part of Chippendale's chair designs. Other stylistic elements occasionally used in Chippendale chair backs include ribband (designs of knotted ribbons) and the ladder (carved horizontal bars).

Carved decorative motifs used in all forms of Chippendale furniture included acanthus leaves, scrolls, ribbons, and interlacing straps. When hardware was present it varied from simple bail handles to elaborately pierced Chinese lattice-design backplates. Arched swan's neck or pierced fretwork pediments added an air of elegance to secretary-bookcases and tall chests. Both straight and curved (ogee) bracket feet were trademarks of this style.

More upholstered furniture was made during this era than ever previously made, but these pieces were the domain of the well-to-do, especially in the United States, where large taxes were levied on imported fabrics.

CHIPPENDALE-STYLE FURNITURE

Just as many fine, faithful reproductions were made of Queen Anne period furniture, the elegant period Chippendale designs were often left untouched by discriminating furniture designers. Still, though, the Chippendale decorative elements—particularly the pierced chair backs and decorative carved elements used in the overall designs—provided a literal playground for those late-nineteenth- and twentieth-century artisans and craftsmen who couldn't resist trying their hand at "improving" eighteenth-century motifs.

These designers took wonderful, perfectly balanced chair backs and overran them with scrolls and curlicues, rosettes and acanthus motifs. Where one band of carved pierced work was sufficient, they crowded in additional borders of gadrooning. Where a simple carved acanthus leaf was enough, they added two more leaves and a cluster of berries to boot. In other words, too much of a good thing ended up being overkill. Worst of all was the abuse of Chip-

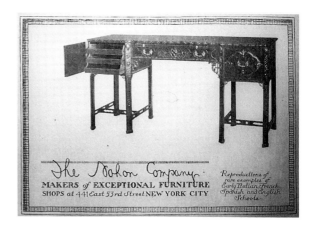

The Mahon Company created excellent-quality pieces that the interior designers often used in their most expensive homes. This Chinese Chippendale server is one such example.

pendale's use of Oriental motifs known as "Chinese Chippendale." (See top photograph, page 117.)

Chinese designs had intrigued Westerners ever since Marco Polo brought back a few trinkets from his travels, especially exquisite open latticework and the pagoda form. Scholarly books on the history of furniture carefully point out that the use of Chinese motifs in furniture originated not with Chippendale but with Sir William Chambers, George I's favorite architect. But Chambers is mostly forgotten while the term "Chinese Chippendale" is part of every interior designer's vocabulary.

When Chippendale incorporated these Eastern motifs into his basically English furniture designs, he did so with restraint. Not so the twentieth-century American furniture makers, who, with the help of the new machines, could whip out lattice patterns made of cheap materials and tack, nail, or glue them onto any straight surface and call the piece "Chinese Chippendale." Cut-out geometric designs embellished drawer fronts, sofa legs, the sides of chests of drawers, and secretary pediments until no flat surface was sacrosanct. One writer described the end result as a "lattice fill-in" resembling "zigzag streaks of lightning." In no time, the easily made, showy "Chinese Chippendale" strip of latticework became as abused as the Jacobean spiral motif.

When *Furniture Design* is such that it remains in the best of taste for generations and emerges triumphant through many cycles of furniture fads extending over several centuries, it is then that superiority of construction reaches its highest aspect of importance.

To go hand in hand with the permanence of its time-tested furniture patterns, the Biggs Antique Company utilizes every lesson from Fifty-Two Years experience to produce *Antiques for Future Generations.*

—From the Biggs of Richmond, Virginia, 1940s catalog

Many companies also hastily created untold numbers of loose adaptations of Chippendale forms so a unified "Chippendale look" could be had throughout the home. For example, the very best designed tables created during the Chippendale era (not necessarily by Chippendale himself—remember, Chippendale's *Directory* was a widely copied pattern book) were supported by a center column or pedestal. During the eighteenth century, Chippendale tabletops and pedestals were simple or elaborate—depending on the customer's taste and wealth. In the twentieth century, Chippendale-style tables turned up in every conceivable design from dining room tables (usually the legs were too heavy) to coffee tables (remember, those originated in the 1920s).

The one room that seems to have escaped the "Chippendale look" was the bedroom. The beds of the period had tall posts and were canopied. They were grand, imposing, and heavily draped. The twentieth-century twelve-by-fifteen foot bedroom just could not accommodate furniture of such proportions. But of course, if you took a little fretwork and a pagoda motif and stuck it on a twin-size headboard, voilà!

Probably the most copied of all of Chippendale's designs was a piece that was both appropriate and suitable to virtually any room in the twentieth-century house—the ubiquitous Chip-

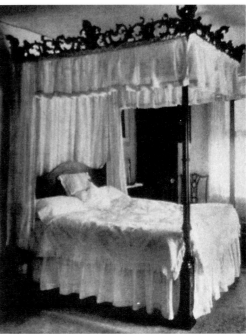

It took a mammoth room like the bedroom featured in Good Furniture (right) or the one at the Swan House (top) in Atlanta to accommodate a true Chippendale-style bed, and so the next best thing was a scaled-down fanciful version (above). (Note the strong similarities between the two fine-quality Chippendale-style beds.) (Swan House photo courtesy of the Atlanta History Center)

pendale-style mirror recognizable by either a C-scroll pediment or a Chinese-style pagoda top. Indeed, Emily Post, writing in *The Personality of a House,* gushed "the long-beaked bird amidst the scrolled 'C's' of his [Chippendale's] name ornamenting his gilt mirror frames, are dreams of Celestial loveliness."

Other pieces—secretaries, china cabinets, and slant-front and writing desks—were all both faithfully copied and bastardized in varying degrees by American reproduction furniture makers. A careful study and analysis of the best, the all-right, and the terribly wrong designs will quickly bring these differences to light.

A richly lacquered Chippendale-style grandfather clock, typical of the finest-quality reproductions made during the first part of the 20th century.

The ubiquitous Chippendale-style mirror—this one with a pagoda top, accompanying a similarly styled console table ideal for the early-20th-century foyer.

No one could ever be at a loss to correctly identify the Chinese Chippendale influence in this reproduction chair!

Even a record player takes on a special pedigree when it is of a "period design," as in the ad for this Chinese Chippendale–style lacquered Columbia Grafonola gramophone.

The Chippendale pierced fretwork on the 18th-century drop-leaf table (above) was first traced from a template and then cut out, carved, and smoothed down by hand. Shown below are Chippendale-motif corner frets created entirely by machine.(Furniture Discovery Center)

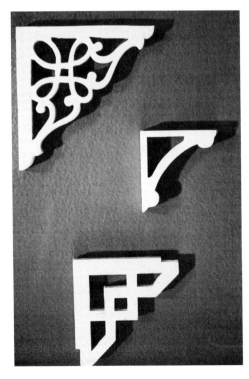

Though period furniture correctly called "Adam" was made in late-18th-century England, the style caught on with great vigor in the United States a century later, thanks to such renderings as this illustration (opposite) from Clarence Cook's The House Beautiful.

The Adam Brothers (Robert and James), 1762–1792

There were four Adam brothers—John, Robert, James, and William—all of whom strongly influenced both English architecture and cabinet-making during the last half of the eighteenth century. Robert left his native Scotland to spend four years studying architecture in Italy, during which time he visited many classical ruins, including Diocletian's palace at Spoleto. Armed with sketches, Robert returned to England where, with his brother James, he developed a classical style that wedded architecture and furniture.

In contrast to the strong and bold Chippendale style, the "Adam style," as it came to be known, was light, refined, and straight-lined. Even large case pieces (secretaries, tall chests, and display cases) had a delicacy about them.

Just as Jacobean furniture is distinguishable by spiral turnings, Queen Anne furniture has cabriole legs and curved lines, and Chippendale furniture is noted for its pierced motifs and boldness, so Adam furniture is quickly recognizable by its distinguishing trait: classically inspired architectural ornamentation, especially festoons, garlands, swags, floral and fruit motifs, ribbons, and even putti.

Sometimes these motifs were carved, other times they were painted on the furniture surfaces or inlaid into the wood. Adam was indelibly influenced by the classical themes he had seen in Italy. He found the gleaming beauty of gilt highlights irresistible. (When re-creating the Adam "look," twentieth-century furniture designers often used white and gold paint rather than expensive gold leaf.)

Adam furniture is distinctive, especially when compared to earlier styles. What is important to

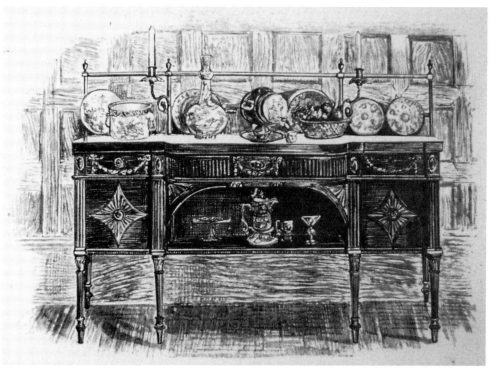

ADAM STYLE

General characteristics	Furniture forms	Ornaments
light, delicate	console tables, sofas	urns and vases
lighter woods, gilt	arm- and side chairs	flowers and garlands
often painted	tables, beds, desks	paterae and ovals
tapering legs	sideboards	ribbons and festoons
slender lines	all varieties of "modern" forms, particularly china cabinets, bedroom suites, and sideboards	beading and moldings
designed to complement a specific architectural-designed room		fluted motif

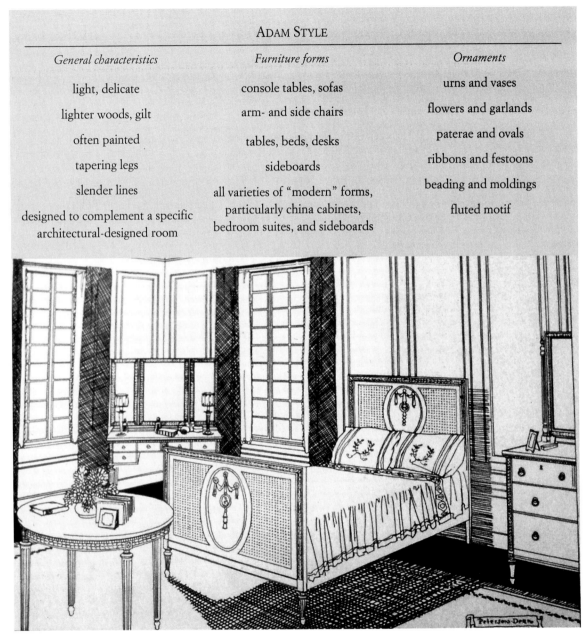

know is that during the period when it was originally made, Adam furniture never caught on in the American colonies. The overall appearance of the furniture was just too light and airy to appeal to the more rugged tastes of the late-eighteenth-century Americans who were accustomed to mahogany furniture—not painted pieces with gilt highlights. But in the first part of the twentieth century the Adam style became the rage in the United States, especially when the designs were slightly modified to have a more informal look in keeping with the American way of life.

ADAM-STYLE FURNITURE

When discussing Adam-style furniture, the ground rule is that the essence of this style is its decoration or ornamentation, not its shape, structure, or form. Just as the American furniture designers thought that by tacking a strip of lattice banding onto a piece of furniture they had created a Chinese Chippendale piece, so they assumed that they could attach a garland swag held up by a couple of classical urns and instantly have a piece of Adam-style furniture. Unfortunately, this is what they did, especially on bedroom furniture.

Bedroom furniture based on the preceding historical styles—Jacobean, Queen Anne, and Chippendale—was overbearing in the bedrooms. But the more delicate Adam motifs, especially combined with painted surfaces—white enamel was the favorite—were appropriate and attractive. Interestingly, many of the adaptive reproduction Adam-style pieces have a distinctly fresh, modern look when placed in a brightly painted 1900s room complete with bold and colorful drapery and upholstery patterns.

Another favorite design brought forward from the Adam period and adapted to the twentieth century was the pairing up of a console table and mirror. Remember, originally Robert Adam was interested in architecture. The only reason he and his brother, James, became involved in furniture design was so a room's furnishings would be in harmony with the interiors they had designed. During the eighteenth century a pair of graceful, oval-shaped mirrors hung over a charming pair of richly detailed semicircular tables were stunning in a country manor ballroom. Take just one of each and scale it down to fit the modern foyer or the space between two living room windows, and the result was magical.

On this fine-quality American-made Adam-style console table and accompanying mirror scenes of romantic ruins and the general decorative ornament—especially the griffins—are strongly Italian-influenced.

Hepplewhite Period Furniture, 1760–1815

Working in England during the same, overlapping time frame as the Adam were two other furniture designers, Hepplewhite and Sheraton. Their traditional mahogany furniture was more to the liking of the Americans who largely shunned the Adam look.

Little is known about George Hepplewhite except that his wife, Dame Alice Hepplewhite, was probably largely responsible for the perpetu-

Fine interior designers loved the light, airy feeling of the Adam style captured in reproductions like the sofa shown above, covered in appropriate upholstery with an urn and garland pattern. Here (left) is a wonderfully put together designer-decorated room that uses the Adam oval motif in the rug, center table, screen, and sconces, as well as the architectural wall panels and ceiling. Pictured at top is a true Adam room, 20th-century style, complete with complementary, urn-decorated, English Wedgwood accessories.

Take basic pieces, attach a strong Adam-style motif—in this case garlands and an urn—paint the pieces white, and you have an entire Adamesque 1920s bedroom suite!

I'll admit that it is fun to comb the old books and magazines, catalogs and ads, looking for just the right illustration to complement the text. When I saw this "Adam" chair (above), I had to laugh out loud. Doesn't the back motif remind you of either tennis rackets or oversized golf tees? I doubt if any 18th-century furniture designer would ever have come up with a chair that looks like this one!

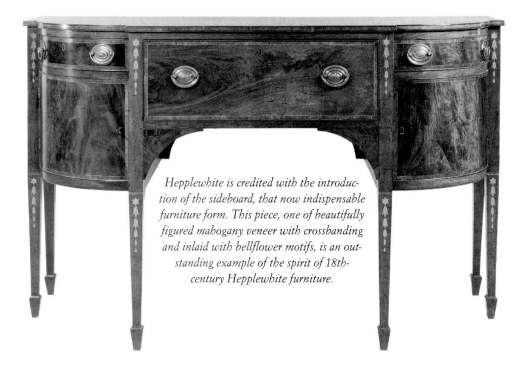

Hepplewhite is credited with the introduction of the sideboard, that now indispensable furniture form. This piece, one of beautifully figured mahogany veneer with crossbanding and inlaid with bellflower motifs, is an outstanding example of the spirit of 18th-century Hepplewhite furniture.

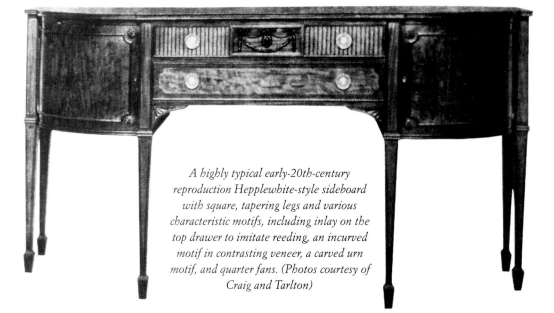

A highly typical early-20th-century reproduction Hepplewhite-style sideboard with square, tapering legs and various characteristic motifs, including inlay on the top drawer to imitate reeding, an incurved motif in contrasting veneer, a carved urn motif, and quarter fans. (Photos courtesy of Craig and Tarlton)

ation of his designs. It was she who published his volumes of *The Cabinet Maker and Upholsterer's Guide* in 1788, 1789, and 1794, and who continued his work under the name A. Hepplewhite and Company. There are many similarities between the Adams' and Hepplewhite's designs, as you will see when comparing the illustrations of each maker. Hepplewhite, too, was influenced by foreign vogues—he was a particular fan of Louis XVI furniture. However, Hepplewhite used mahogany, still the most favored wood, combined with rosewood, tulipwood, and satinwood to give his pieces a stronger, sturdier feeling than the Adams' furniture.

Though Hepplewhite and the Adams used many of the same decorative motifs—most often *inlaid*, not carved, urns, swags, paterae—Hepplewhite's designs were more adaptable to the homes of the day on both sides of the Atlantic than were the Adams' pieces, which were specifically coordinated to a room's design from ceiling to floor. Many of Hepplewhite's designs also blended well with earlier Queen Anne and Chippendale pieces. This adaptability factor made Hepplewhite's designs some of the most widely reproduced by the American furniture companies a century later.

The easiest way to recognize Hepplewhite-style furniture is by the legs, which are almost without exception square and tapering. The exceptions are the occasional round and tapered legs, but these types of legs are mostly used with the typical Hepplewhite back, which will be discussed next. Hepplewhite's square chair legs most often ended in a spade foot, or were sometimes cuffed, and could also be reeded.

Hepplewhite chairs have four types of backs. The shield shape is most characteristic

Note the many differences between the lines of the 18th-century Hepplewhite secretary-bookcase and the Chippendale one illustrated on page 115. (Photo courtesy of Craig and Tarlton)

HEPPLEWHITE STYLE

General characteristics	*Furniture forms*	*Ornaments*
delicate, slender lines	tambour desks, sofas	inlay predominates
mahogany or walnut	arm- and side chairs,	crossbanding
square, tapering legs	china cabinets, beds, sideboards	lyres, quarter fans, bellflowers, swags
shield-shaped backs	Pembroke tables	
outwardly curving or spade feet	various adaptive forms, especially dressing tables and low tables	Prince of Wales plume, reeding
contrasting veneers		incurved panels

of the style, but backs were also hoop, heart, or oval shaped. Just as the carved backs of Chippendale chairs are distinctive, so the carved backs of Hepplewhite's chairs have a look all their own. The favorite motifs were inverted bellflower husks, wheat, lyres, urns, and of course swag and garland motifs. The Prince of Wales feathers (three plumes tied together) was another popular theme and one greatly copied later.

Perhaps Hepplewhite's greatest contribution to furniture design was the styling of the sideboard as we know it today. Before this time,

The two most popular styles of Hepplewhite chair backs are the heart shape and the shield shape. The heart-shaped back chairs with carved Prince of Wales plume motif (above) are of fine quality, while the shield-back chairs (below), with another commonly used Hepplewhite design, the classical urn, were made by a less-fine company. The rocker is definitely out of character for a period chair. (Top photo by David Nicolay, courtesy of Neal Auction Company)

Hepplewhite pieces inherently have a lighter feeling because of their slim, tapering feet and lighter colored wood. Twentieth-century furniture designers took advantage of this scale and look and slimmed case pieces down even more to fit into smaller modern homes, as in the two china cabinets at left.

An unusual reproduction Hepplewhite-style sideboard adapted from the earlier sideboard form that had large cabinet sections flanking a center serving table. Notice the urns in the ovals and garlands.

Opposite: Many liberties were taken with Hepplewhite chair designs. Here is one such example, a lacquered chinoiserie scene characteristic of the Queen Anne and Chippendale periods embellishing a basically correct Hepplewhite-style chair back.

Here is yet another unusual reproduction sideboard that most likely should be referred to as Chippendale-style. It is included here so you can see how the popular Hepplewhite decorative motif, the garland and flowers, was haphazardly added at the center of the top drawers—just because!

serving tables with or without drawers were standard dining room pieces. Sometimes large ends for storing wine, china, linens, or silver were designed to flank the serving table, but these were separate. Hepplewhite made a sideboard to accommodate the concept of a serving table and to have the storage space of the ends all in one distinct form.

The later nineteenth century was also a time for new table designs. This was largely precipitated by two factors. First was the evolution of having a greater number of separate rooms in a house to accommodate specific purposes than there had previously been. Second was the burgeoning of the middle-class merchant society that could afford houses and furnishings. These two changes were among many that coincided to create a whole new lifestyle that gave rise to new furniture forms. Tables of all sorts were churned out in the Hepplewhite style: card, serving, work,

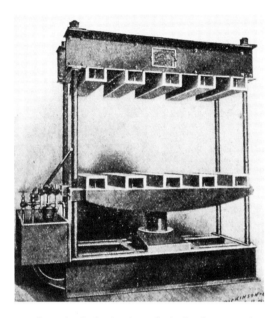

The
Snyder Line

this season includes a surprisingly large addition of new designs in high grade dining suites at medium prices. These suites, in period styles, are made in a variety of woods and finishes, including American Walnut.

Snyder Furniture Co.
Grand Rapids,   Michigan

At our display in the Manufacturers Building:
J. W. SHANK & SON.   H. J. WOHLFORD.
A. T. KINGSBURY.   O. K. WILCOX.
J. D. MISKILL.

It only took a little glue from the hydraulic press (above) to attach machine-created Hepplewhite motifs—urns, garlands, ovals, etc.—to one piece (below), or to a whole suite (left). Though the purist may long for hand-carved ornaments, as new ways of creating ornamentation of plastic and even photographic images become commonplace on the furniture of the 21st century, these mass-manufactured old reproduction pieces look better and better to us.

Pembroke, and dressing tables were among the most popular. At the same time, many of the larger, more ponderous forms like the secretary-bookcase and chest-on-chest, were scaled down to become more delicate in size and appearance. On these last two pieces, a splay leg was often used, adding a graceful ending to the form.

HEPPLEWHITE-STYLE FURNITURE

When the twentieth-century furniture designer sketched the outline of the Hepplewhite chair, his eye surely zeroed in on the chair back. Out came his protractor and his imagination. The space had to be filled and the new cutting machines in the factories made it possible to mass-produce almost any design. And there were so many designs to choose from. By now you are familiar enough with them to list them yourself: swags, bellflowers, urns, bows, ribbons, and so on. So it is in the chair backs that the greatest liberty was taken with Hepplewhite's basic style.

The new twentieth-century table forms were also given a Hepplewhite look by utilizing these motifs. This time, though, the decoration was as often added by inserting mass-produced inlay in these shapes and designs as it was by gluing or nailing on a carved decoration. In all fairness, though, remember back to chapter 1. Even the early cabinetmakers had used templates, jigs, and stencils to facilitate the inlay process. The sad state of affairs, if I may look ahead to the furniture of the future, is that in this computer age, photo-processing techniques are sometimes being used to create the appearance of inlay on today's newly made Hepplewhite pieces rather than involving the expense and trouble of using actual contrasting woods. Is it any wonder that the well-made old reproductions are coming into their own?

Sheraton Period Furniture, 1785–1815

Thomas Sheraton, the last cabinetmaker of England's "Golden Age of Furniture Making," moved from northern England to London in 1790, most likely to publish his work *The Cabinet Maker's and Upholsterer's Drawing Book.* Unlike Hepplewhite, about whom so little is known, we know that Sheraton was an extremely energetic man, for not only was he a cabinetmaker, he also was an author, bookseller, publisher, and teacher. Yet he died in 1806, poverty-stricken and disillusioned. Apparently, like many multitalented people, he lacked the ability to focus his energies and so was never really successful in any of his enterprises. It was only after his death that Sheraton's designs actually gained widespread popularity.

Like his contemporaries, Sheraton preferred straight lines, but to these he added a sweep here and a curve there. It was during Sheraton's lifetime that a fancy for lighter woods developed, and many of his designs were produced during this period in lighter satinwood and even such rare, exotic woods as tulipwood, kingwood, rosewood, zebrawood, amboyna, and thuya.

But the single characteristic the general public associates with Sheraton's designs is his use of slender, rounded legs that were often reeded and tapered. In lieu of then adding on a foot, Sheraton usually continued the leg line down or splayed it outward.

Because Sheraton and Hepplewhite were working during the same years and in the same general fashion environment, there are many similarities between their designs. By and large though, by comparing this written explanation of Sheraton's designs with the illustrations provided, I think the differences between the two styles are evident. In addition to the different leg styles, Sheraton-type chairs had very characteristic squared backs in contrast to Hepplewhite oval or shield designs. Sheraton chair backs were typically very low and open in appearance, sometimes with a broad, shaped rail at the top. Horizontal and vertical bars, diagonal lattices, vases, and lyres were his favorite motifs.

On the other common forms of Sheraton period furniture—upholstered sofas, chests of drawers, sideboards, tables of all sorts, secretaries, and cabinets—the round, reeded legs are immediate giveaways. One note about sideboards: While Hepplewhite is given credit for conceiving the popular serpentine-shaped sideboard, Sheraton sideboards are more often bow-fronted or straight across. Again, the illustrations will help with these distinctions. Credit is also given to Sheraton for designing the kidney-shaped table, as well as for concealing secret drawers in furniture.

The single embellishment most often associated with Sheraton's pieces is the reeded column. This is the same visual motif Sheraton used as the basis for his leg, but it was also used to form arms on Sheraton sofas and armchairs and as a decorative motif on sideboards, chests of drawers, mirrors, and tables.

SHERATON-STYLE FURNITURE

When compared to the more elegant Chippendale and Queen Anne furniture styles or the more delicate Adam and Hepplewhite styles, Sheraton furniture is really a straightforward, no-fuss sort of design. Granted, modern furniture designers freely scaled down the dimensions of Sheraton period pieces, especially large cupboards and wide chests, to fit twentieth-century homes. But the lines of the furniture were often faithfully followed. The designers went awry when, rather than leaving the surfaces plain, or decorated with just the reeded column motif, they attached the urns and swags, bellflowers and ovals favored by Adam and Hepplewhite.

A Word About Federal Furniture

In the United States, the sweeping movement toward democracy and establishing self-government came in the 1770–1800 era—the years of the British-originated Adam, Hepplewhite, and Sheraton periods. I have already touched on why Adam furniture designs were not as well received on this side of the Atlantic as they were in England. But Hepplewhite and Sheraton designs

The reeded, rounded, tapering legs of the three period furniture forms shown on these pages are instant indicators that these are Sheraton pieces. But don't just look at the legs. Admire the beautiful figured mahogany used in the table and sideboard to break up what otherwise could be just a plain, uninteresting flat surface. The graceful and comfortable Sheraton sofa form remains one of today's most popular shapes. (Photos courtesy of Craig and Tarlton)

SHERATON STYLE

General characteristics	Furniture forms	Ornaments
simplicity of line	pedestal tables	elaborate turning and carving, especially of the legs
mahogany or walnut	sofas, settees	fluting and reeding
round, tapering legs	arm- and side chairs	crossbars and lyres
horizontal and vertical chair backs	sewing, work, and dressing tables	more painted furniture
raised or splayed feet	because more furniture forms were made during the period, there are fewer out-of-period pieces	

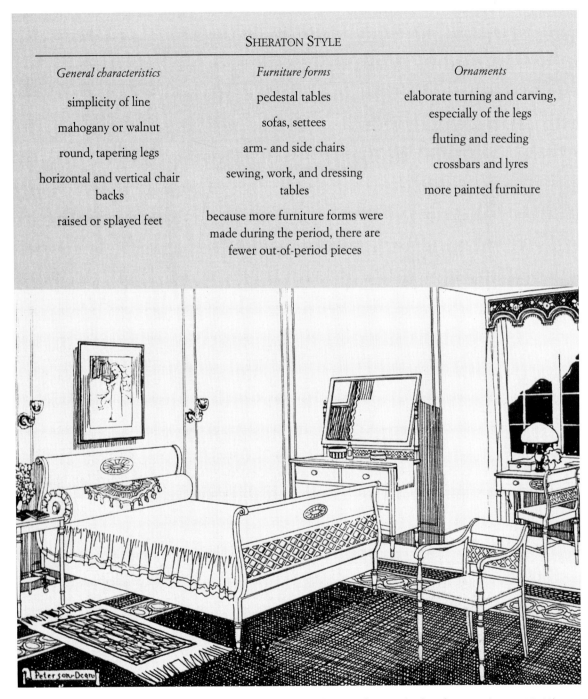

By comparing the illustrations on these pages to the comparable ones for Hepplewhite furniture (pages 128–31) many similarities are visible. The only distinction that can truly help differentiate the two styles is that of the rounded leg characteristic of the Sheraton style.

SIDEBOARD
Sheraton Adaptation.
Crotch Mahogany.
Antique Finish.
Height, 44 inches. Width, 72 inches.

CHAIR
Sheraton Adaptation.
Crotch Mahogany.
Antique Finish.
Upholstered Slip Seat.

ARM CHAIR
Sheraton Adaptation.
Crotch Mahogany.
Antique Finish.
Upholstered Slip Seat.

were extensively copied in America's cabinet shops. To move away from the English association with these forms that were given their own style in the United States, the broad-sweeping term "Federal" is often used in lieu of Hepplewhite and Sheraton in the same way that we describe objects as "Chippendale" rather than "Georgian." For this reason, the term "Federal" often may be used interchangeably with Hepplewhite and Sheraton. Remember though, if the piece in question is decorated with an eagle or Columbia, or another American symbol, it is best to refer to it as "Federal."

This ad for the very fine company Erskine-Danforth captures the national pride that was responsible for dubbing furniture made during the last years of the 18th century "Federal."

Just as Hepplewhite sideboards and Queen Anne chairs were the most frequently copied forms of their period, so the Sheraton sofa, with its unobtrusive wooden frame and the restrained, unified look of the shaped, reeded legs and arms, is among the most-often-reproduced classical furniture pieces.

Here are two different versions of adaptive Sheraton-style double beds dating from the 1920 era. Painted furniture was increasingly popular during the Sheraton period, and 20th-century furniture companies followed suit. The painted bed (above) is a prime example of a designer sticking on unneeded whorls and doodads just to put them there.

Empire Period Furniture, 1815–1850

Empire furniture had barely passed out of fashion when the first rumblings of the machines that would make American reproduction furniture began. At its best, early-period Empire furniture is extraordinarily high-style, with highly polished finishes, sweeping grand lines, and exotic classical motifs—palmettes, griffins, caryatids, cornu-

copias and serpents, to name a few. At its worst, later-period Empire furniture is dark and gloomy, oversized and starkly plain. And somewhere in between there are beautifully scaled and wonderfully carved pieces associated with Duncan Phyfe's New York workshop that were often more "Sheraton" than "Empire."

The bulk of Empire furniture is most quickly identified by its massive proportions and ma-

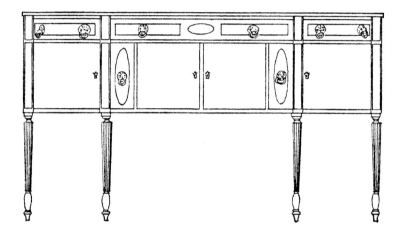

These two sideboards show the vivid contrast between the lighter, more delicate Sheraton pieces of circa 1800 and the much heavier, ponderous American Empire pieces of twenty to forty years later. The Sheraton sideboard (above) is quickly identifiable by its reeded, rounded, tapering legs. The Empire one (below) is distinguished by the deep cabinet section that extends almost to the floor and by the strongly figured mahogany veneer.

hogany-veneered surface. Chests of drawers that traditionally had been "waist high" now were "chest high." Sideboards that usually had one tier of drawers above a ten- to fifteen-inch cabinet section were now designed to have the drawer section above a cabinet section that just skirted the floor (opposite, bottom). Secretaries no longer had lift-down writing slants. Instead, the large top drawer opened and the front panel dropped down to make a writing surface.

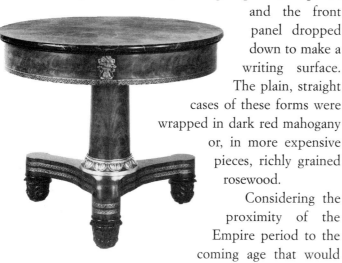

The plain, straight cases of these forms were wrapped in dark red mahogany or, in more expensive pieces, richly grained rosewood.

Considering the proximity of the Empire period to the coming age that would mass-produce earlier styles, the logical assumption might be that enough period Empire furniture would still be around not to merit the making of reproductions. Ironically, Empire reproductions were turned out by the gross and were immensely popular with the public. After all, much of the old furniture was now dingy and often in poor condition, while the new was fresh and yet had the look of the old.

High-style Empire furniture is grand in its gilded glory. This center table (left), with its stenciled banding and basket of flowers, applied foliage ring at the bottom of the pedestal, and acanthus carved feet, has great personality. So has the pier table (below) with carved cornucopias at the

apron. But there are only a few of these pieces compared to the tremendous number of simpler pier tables (like the one at top) and chests (the chest at left is a 1920s reproduction). (Center table photo courtesy of Craig and Tarlton; pier tables photo by David Nicolay, courtesy of Neal Auction Company)

EMPIRE STYLE		
General characteristics	*Furniture forms*	*Ornaments*
strong, straight lines	large desks	the figuring of the wood is often used in place of embellishment
dark, figured mahogany veneer	commodious sofas and chairs	
heavy legs and feet	china cabinets and buffets, sideboards	pedestal or columns
curving, rolled-over, or scroll shapes	sleigh beds	some gilding
paw and scroll feet	all sorts of tables and small stands Like Golden Oak furniture, any large, oversized, heavily grained mahogany piece is often called "Empire."	cornucopia, fruit, and foliage carving

EMPIRE-STYLE FURNITURE

So little high-style (or neoclassical) Empire furniture such as the elaborate pier table on the bottom right of page 143 was copied by American furniture companies that it really does not merit discussion here. The style and design was too sophisticated, too rarified for the masses. Rather, the companies concentrated on what they knew they could sell—the pieces the Jones' and Smiths' grandparents had had in their homes—the big, the bulky, and the dark late Empire pieces, with a few more delicate "Duncan Phyfe" designs thrown in.

The companies had a field day with this style. The straight frames were little more than machine-sawn boards with surfaces of thin (read inexpensive) sheets of veneer. The pieces had originally been made just when the machines born of the Industrial Revolution were being developed. Now, just a few years later, the machines had been perfected. Making Empire furniture was a piece of cake—especially when the pieces were scaled down to twentieth-century ceiling heights and room proportions.

The new machinery made it simple to cut large sheets of veneer and glue it to straight-board cases to create reproductions of the pieces Granny had.

It can be difficult to distinguish Empire period pieces from fine measured reproductions. The two sofas shown above are both period pieces. The one at the top is simpler in styling, with its reeded frame and brass caster paw-motif feet. The other, with its scrolled-over crest rail and arms carved with rosettes and foliage decoration, plus its carved paw feet and foliage spilling out of the cornucopias, is much more exuberant. But these basic styles were copied a million times over, as seen in the two reproductions below, and sometimes so well that occasionally the fabric has to be pulled back to prove (or disprove) period construction. (Period photos courtesy of Craig and Tarlton)

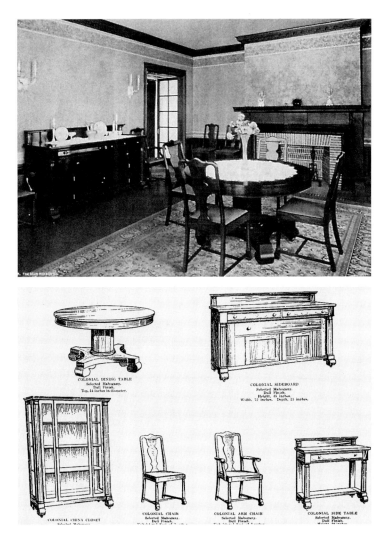

The Victorian Era, 1840–1900

The Industrial Revolution and the Victorian Era debuted and developed together. Victoria reigned as queen from 1837 to 1901. The turn-of-the-century return to classical forms was, in part, in reaction to the elaborate styles of the Victorian era. There was simply no reason for the furniture companies to make copies of styles that no one liked—during the early boom days of American-made reproduction furniture, that is. A few years later, in the 1940s and 1950s, *its* time had come, but that's a subject for another book.

Empire furniture was a real favorite of the reproduction furniture companies during the 1900–1930 era. The problem noted in this book is that they often dubbed Empire-style furniture "Colonial." This "Colonial" dining room set, shown as a sketch and arranged in a room, actually comprises two styles. The table, sideboard, and china cabinet are all Empire-style adaptations, while the chairs combine an Empire-style leg and foot with a modified Queen Anne–style backsplat. Why combine or mix the two styles? Why not? It was easy to cut out mass numbers of those backsplats and they always look good.

It would be some time before the Victorian styles once again found public favor. During the first part of the 20th century such highly carved, floral-decorated pieces were out of fashion. The resurgence of the Victorian era blossomed in the late 1940s. (Photo by David Nicolay, courtesy of Neal Auction Company)

The curvaceous lines and rich silk fabrics of the French Louis styles have always been popular and strongly influenced many of the Victorian furniture designs. At the Voigt House in Grand Rapids, the American-made Louis XV–style table made circa 1920 by Johnson-Handley-Johnson is often mistaken as a European, probably French—but not American—reproduction.

The Louis Periods

LOUIS XV, 1715–1774

Worldwide, no other style of furniture has been so esteemed as that made during the reign of Louis XV. It was a paradoxical time in history; one brilliantly described in *Modern Period American Furniture* as when "vice was refined, licentiousness was genteel, immorality was garbed in the cloak of elegance." Nonetheless, it was also a time of exquisite, unequaled craftsmanship and sophisticated taste.

The furniture of the day was at the same time luxurious and substantial, sensuous and sturdy, appealing and magnificent. One word defines the basic Louis XV style: curves. From the

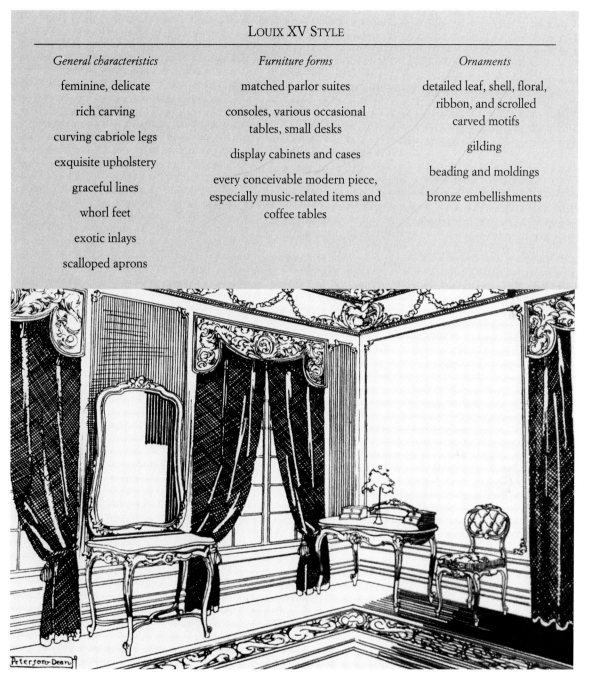

General characteristics	Furniture forms	Ornaments

LOUIX XV STYLE

General characteristics

feminine, delicate

rich carving

curving cabriole legs

exquisite upholstery

graceful lines

whorl feet

exotic inlays

scalloped aprons

Furniture forms

matched parlor suites

consoles, various occasional tables, small desks

display cabinets and cases

every conceivable modern piece, especially music-related items and coffee tables

Ornaments

detailed leaf, shell, floral, ribbon, and scrolled carved motifs

gilding

beading and moldings

bronze embellishments

rounded backs of the chairs and scrolled-over arms of the chaises, to the ever-present cabriole legs and circular motifs and ruffly ornaments, to the gilded surfaces that caught and reflected the sunlight and firelight, every part of each piece had a subtle motion.

LOUIS XV–STYLE FURNITURE

All of this was just too much for most modern-day craftsmen to emulate. Add to the inherent formality of the pieces their glitz and delicate femininity, and the audience was limited. Yet the style had a place in the sophisticated drawing rooms and bedrooms of New York, Washington, Palm Beach, and San Francisco. In those cities, houses of the wealthy literally dripped in the French-style furniture made by a handful of companies and craftsmen.

But as so often happens with the most expensive goods, a low-end demand for the same style developed, and so "faux Louis XV" became a fad. The only way to describe the quickly assem-

bled, inexpensive twentieth-century knock-offs of Louis XV furniture is "in name only," for not only were these lines made of inferior materials, the pieces themselves lacked the robust spirit and the rich attention to detail that gave the style its character and charm—all of which explains why there are so few well-made and so many cheaply made American reproductions of Louis XV furniture around.

LOUIS XVI, 1774–1793, AND THE LATER COPIES

Much the same can be said for the "other Louis style," Louis XVI. The furniture of the period was beautiful and beautifully made. For identifi-

Again, turn your attention to the legs. Louis XV furniture is always recognizable by its cabriole leg. Beyond that, the style is distinguished from the Louis XVI style by its more delicate scale and appearance, and its curving lines. Compare these three reproduction pieces to the Louis XVI ones pictured on the bottom of page 152 and 154.

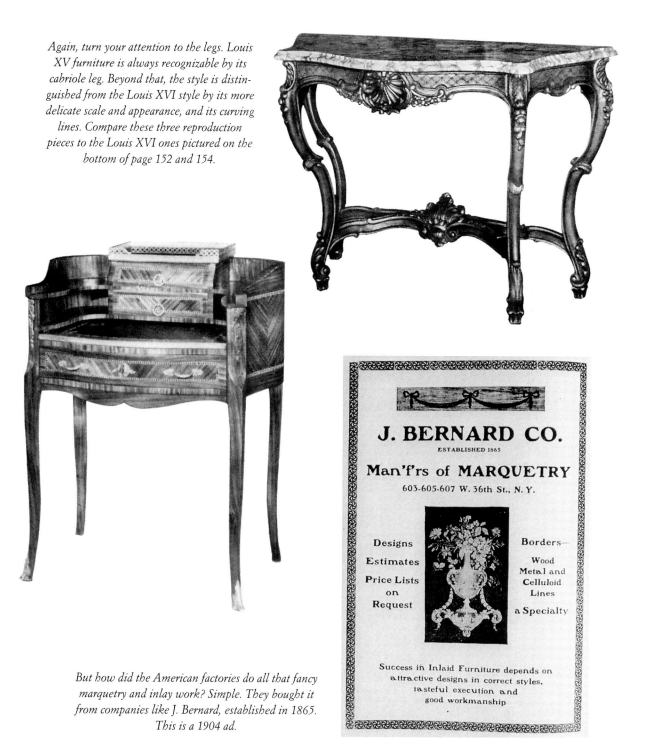

But how did the American factories do all that fancy marquetry and inlay work? Simple. They bought it from companies like J. Bernard, established in 1865. This is a 1904 ad.

Just as many fine American-manufactured pieces made in English style, like the Jacobean-style joint stool illustrated on page 99, are often mistaken as English-made, so most people seeing a Louis XV–style bombé chest or commode like this one would assume it has to be French—probably 18th century! Surprisingly, it is circa 1930 and American-made.

cation purposes, its basic form was no longer curving, but more linear with straight-fronted chests, rectangular-backed sofas, and round tapering legs replacing the curvaceous cabriole legs. Its greater simplicity made it not only easier to reproduce but almost more suitable to the twentieth-century home. A piece or two of Louis XVI furniture added an air of elegant sophistication rather than excessive show.

If, when looking at the illustrations, you sense a strong resemblance between Louis XVI designs and those of the Adam brothers, it is because they share many of the same elements—from the architectural motifs used to embellish the surfaces to the round, tapering legs.

And should you have trouble distinguishing between Louis XV and Louis XVI, remember, the basic Louis XV contours can be loosely compared to the curving lines of English Queen Anne furniture, while the basic Louis XVI form is

The straight sides and legs characteristic of Louis XVI furniture are a marked contrast to the curving lines of Louis XV furniture.

LOUIS XVI STYLE

General characteristics	Furniture forms	Ornaments
open, refined, sophisticated	all sorts of tables—gaming, dressing, long console, and end	fluting and reeding
formal, straight lines	matched upholstered suites	flowers, torches, wreaths, and bows
round or straight legs	all varieties of "modern pieces," especially painted bedroom suites	beaded motifs
classical in feeling		bands of interlacing circles and scrolls
graceful without being fussy and feminine		

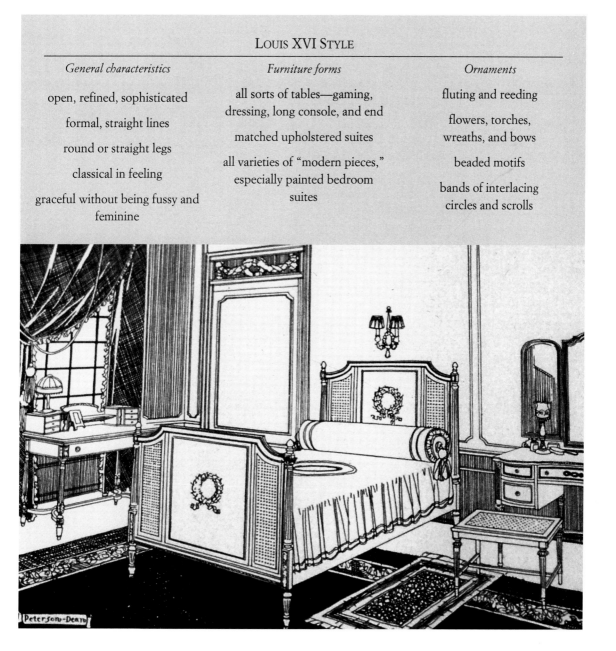

vaguely reminiscent of the Adam and Sheraton lines. In fact, by the time the American furniture companies finished fiddling around with the Louis XVI original styles and had placed the floral and swag motifs, ovals and ribbons, where they wanted them, attached round, tapering legs on each piece, and finished them off in white enamel paint, only the name given to the line could distinguish whether you were looking at an Adam, Sheraton, or Louis XVI adaptation.

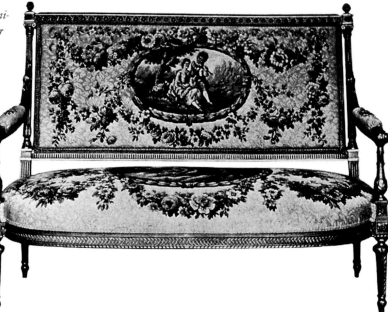

Exquisite Louis-style furniture was ideally suited for the home or pied-à-terre of fabulously wealthy Americans, and of those who wished they were. Pieces like this Louis XVI settee with expensive tapestry upholstery gave an incomparable air of well-traveled sophistication and refinement. This room view incorporates the Louis XVI style into the surroundings.

Pictured here are two versions of enameled Louis XVI–style bedroom suites for the 1915 home. The grouping shown
above is fully embellished with garland swags and has reeded, round legs.
A simpler adaptation is the straight-legged and less-decorated version pictured below.

By the 1940s, the choices were clear-
cut: traditional or modern. These
room views gleaned from old magazine features and advertisements
show the contrasts between the
"looks" of the day. Those people who
loved the richness and warmth of
wood and the various shapes and
ornamentation of time-tested styles—
curved and flaring legs, turned chair
backs, carved bedposts, and so on—
found little to admire in the heavily
upholstered and plain, monotonous
surfaces of the new furniture. See also
the comparable, but oh so different,
room views on pages 158 and 159.

Epilogue

J ust as some argue that the demise of "true" antiques came with the onset of the Industrial Revolution in the 1830–1840 era, so a case can be made that the combined effects of the Great Depression and World War II brought about the downfall of American reproduction furniture.

During the 1870–1920 era, many new styles had been introduced. We've looked briefly at some of these—Eastlake, Mission, Thonet, Golden Oak, and Art Nouveau. By and large, though, once they had had their day the pieces in these styles were either disposed of or relegated to attics, basements, and garages. That's why, in those styles that are once again popular, in particular Mission and Golden Oak, collectors seek out and pay high prices for genuinely old pieces (not later copies) that are in their original condition.

Contemporary and Classical Compatibles

But some of the innovative styles that appeared in the late 1920s and 1930s had greater staying power. What happened during that epoch was

summed up by the 1937 "New Edition With Supplement on Modern Decoration" of *The Practical Book of Interior Design*.

The first 451 pages of the book remained unchanged from its popular 1919 edition. The "Modern Decoration" supplement was just tacked on at the end. But what truth it spoke, and in such an entertaining manner!

Much of the early modernist furniture was ugly, angular, absurd and utterly impractical. There were bedsteads so heavy that it would take a derrick or a corps of movers to budge them; they were insanitary because they were raised far enough from the floor to allow dust to collect but not far enough to enable a maid to insert a vacuum cleaner or even to clean with a long-handled brush or mop. There were elephantine sofas, so low and so deep-seated, that you were very nearly sitting on the floor; when you wished to rise, there was no way of getting any purchase with your feet and you had to aid the scramble with your hands. Fat people sometimes got stuck and had to be hauled up by anyone else who happened to be present. There were upholstered chairs so

Some called it "streamlined." Some called it "modern." But no one could call the new style of furniture "warm," "inviting," or "homey."

cumbersome and weighty that it took several people to move them and they had to "stay put" where they were, whether you wished to sit there or not. Nearly all of these were of uncompromising, angular contours that suggested anything but physical comfort. At the other extreme, there were ugly contraptions called chairs, made of gas-piping and canvas, that were warranted to take a first prize for supreme discomfort.

Those aberrations, fortunately, are nearly all things of the past. Square-shaped furniture has out-lived its brief vogue and much of the newer modern furniture exhibits a distinct break from "square" conventions along with a marked tendency towards subtlety of line. The designers of modern furniture have learned to contrive both cabinetwork and seating furniture combining the graces of seemliness, comfort and practicality. The chromium-plated metal furniture, with leather or woven-material seats, backs and arms, is really comfortable to sit in and much of it is of at least inoffensive appearance.

It is as true in the late 1990s as it was in the late 1930s that style, material, and comfort are the essential ingredients of successful furniture.

Today, the glass-and-chrome display cabinets and Parsons tables, just to mention two "modern" styles that evolved during that era, remain as popular as they were when they were introduced.

Not only were these pieces eye-catchers and practical for the modern lifestyle, they were skillfully mixed with antiques and antique reproductions by the interior decorators of the day.

The February 1932 issue of *House & Garden* showcased glass furniture under the heading of "a coming style . . . mirrored by furniture that sparkles." The spread included a mirrored writing desk accompanied by the editorial comment, "Furniture of glass, a glittering new note we owe to modernism, is quite as charming in a period room as in a purely contemporary setting." In a word, at last the old and the new styles often complemented one another. The new look did not threaten American-made reproduction furniture, but the Depression and World War II certainly did.

The Great Depression

A century earlier, with the coming of the new technology, many small furniture makers unable to afford the equipment that would have made it possible to turn out furniture rapidly were forced

to close down. Other shops continued to make pieces by hand with the intent of creating a better product, only to find their furniture too expensive for the suddenly financially crippled and dwindling customers.

So it was with the coming of the crash that many small furniture companies, unable to meet their payrolls and expenses, were forced to close their operations. Other companies that had built their businesses on quality by using expensive wood and providing a hand-rubbed finish simply could not sell their expensive products during those hard times.

Survival by Streamlining

Generally, the companies that did manage to survive were most often those which used less expensive materials and produced less expensive pieces of furniture. These were times when everyone settled for second best. The polite word of the day for this was "streamlining."

When a family couldn't afford a new dining room suite, they might be able to swing a breakfast room table and chairs. The family that couldn't afford the corner cupboard they wanted might settle for a coffee table or end table just to cheer up the house.

The once-fat popular home magazines no longer published dream-come-true house plans.

Their pencil-thin issues carried articles on landscaping and do-it-yourself home improvements.

Streamlining went further than the family budget. With the help of machines, furniture companies began streamlining their production costs. A comparison of production methods printed in two catalogs from one company, Albert Grosfeld of New York, says it all.

The 1931 catalog bragged about its reproductions, "which combine the traditional skill and art of European craftsmanship with the requirements of our trade" and could be ordered with special finishes to the walnut frames. Nine years later, in 1940, the Grosfeld catalog announced: "In the face of rising costs of materials and higher wage scales, Grosfeld House upsets all prevailing upward price trends by adopting a startling policy of lower prices. This policy is the direct result of [an] overwhelming demand for a wider selection of Grosfeld House furniture in its now famous 'Limited Income Series.' *Grosfeld House therefore has adjusted production methods throughout its entire factory and resorted to large scale operations which permit these lower prices. . . . The adoption of this policy closes a chapter in the growth of Grosfeld House and opens a new phase of development wherein a highly styled line of furniture authenticated by foremost decorators is now made available to homeowners of average means."* (Emphasis added.)

The tradition of fine-quality reproduction furniture continues to be the preferred look. (Photo courtesy of Kindel)

What lies ahead for reproduction furniture? This early-20th-century ad for Stickley furniture sums it up perfectly: "Old family trees have countless branches but the forefathers' furniture did not multiply." Just as there will never be any more period antiques, neither will there be any more fine old reproduction furniture. That is why the best of the best will be antiques for the next generation.

History Repeats Itself

Do those words sound familiar? With just a few changes these could have been the words of the 1840s, 1870s, 1890s, or the years 1910–19. Throughout modern history the economics of labor and materials, plus the demographics of a growing middle class, have always demanded that furniture manufacturers cut production costs.

And, as history continually shows, the coming of war is the mother of technological invention. World War II was no different from the Civil War or World War I. Men and machines turned out war supplies, not furniture. During the war years, new products and technology evolved. When the war was over, Americans anxious to return to a stable way of life turned their attention to the American dream—their homes.

On the Brink of the Twenty-first Century

Old stuff? To some people, I guess American-made reproduction furniture of bygone years will never be more than old stuff. To me, the furniture itself represents a chapter in our civilization that needs to be preserved and understood.

To a new generation that hates to see a tree cut down when it isn't necessary but at the same time loves a beautiful piece of wood, that spends its time cruising the menu of America Online but loves the earmarks of fine craftsmanship, that takes virtual reality for granted but still cherishes old things—American-made reproduction furniture will be their antiques.

Directory

Furniture Companies Working at the Turn of the Century

There's a second part to the answer Carl Vuncannon of the Furniture Library gave me when I asked him what most people were hoping to learn about American reproduction furniture.

"Companies," Carl told me. "Every day visitors and telephone callers ask, 'Can you tell me when Berkey and Gay were in business? My grandmother had some pieces made by them and I want to know how old they are.'"

It is clear by now that it would be impossible to list every furniture company and when each one was in business. But here, in one place, I have compiled a substantial list of many of the most productive companies working in the early 1900s, the years when American reproductions first appeared in large quantities in the furniture stores across the country.

Few of these companies even exist today. Many merged or were taken over many times and some even changed their names. Most important, remember that only a few of the endless number of companies working during these years can be included in these pages.

The best source for definitive information on furniture companies, as well as every other aspect of the American furniture industry, is *The Grand Rapids Furniture Record,* later known as *The Furniture Record.* The Furniture Library and the Grand Rapids Public Library have original copies. However, Norman Ross Publishing, Inc., has just issued an invaluable microfilm edition that is available for purchase or through larger libraries.

A. B. Chair Company
Charlotte, Mich.
chairs

Acme Kitchen Furniture
Company
Chattanooga, Tenn.
kitchen tables, wardrobes, separate dressers, mantel beds

Adler Veneer Seat Company
Brooklyn, N.Y.
parlor, library and smokers' tables, gilt chairs, veneer seatings

Ahnapee Furniture Company
Algoma, Wis.
chamber suites, odd dressers, commodes

Aimone Manufacturing Company
New York, N.Y.
bedroom, dining, library, hall and fancy furniture in mahogany and inlaid

Air Line Manufacturing Company
Port Norfolk, Va.
library, kitchen, drop-leaf, center, extension, and dining tables

W. S. Allan Manufacturing
Company
Whitney's Point, N.Y.
sideboards, china closests, ladies' desks

Allegany Furniture Company
Cumberland, Md.
chiffoniers, dressers, bedroom suites, cheap and medium*
oak goods

American Cabinet Company
Holland, Mich.
bedroom furniture

American Dining Room Furniture
Company
Martinsville, Va.
bed and dining room suites

American Furniture Company
Batesville, Ind.
chamber suites, odd dressers, chiffoniers

American Veneer Company
New Orange, N.J.
settees, etc.

Anderson Furniture Company
Clinton, Iowa
tables, sideboards, chiffoniers

Arbenz Furniture Company
Chillicothe, Ohio
sideboards, buffets, chiffoniers, and dressers in oak and mahogany

Athens Furniture Company
Athens, Pa.
chamber suites, chiffoniers, and sideboards

Atlantic Furniture Company
Baltimore, Md.
chamber suites, chiffoniers, sideboards, and hat racks

Atlas Parlor Furniture Company
Chicago, Ill.
parlor furniture, frames, etc.

Atlas Table Company
Lexington, N.C.
center, extension, and kitchen tables

Bagby Furniture Company
Baltimore, Md.
chamber suites, hall racks, wardrobes, buffets, tables, chairs, and bedsteads

Bailey-Jones Company
Jamestown, N.Y.
parlor, library, bedroom, directors' and ladies' sewing tables

Baker Furniture Factories
Allegan, Mich.
bedroom and dining room suites

Balkwill and Patch Furniture
Company
Chicago, Ill.
odd dressers, chiffonicrs, washstands, ladies' dressing tables

Ballman Cabinet Company
Cincinnati, Ohio
fancy furniture

John Barnutz
Brooklyn, N.Y.
dining, corner, odd, arm, and hall chairs; dining, library, parlor, sewing, and dressing tables; rockers and settees

Berkey and Gay Furniture
Company
Grand Rapids, Mich.
dining room, library, living room furniture

*Note: When value assessments (cheap, medium, fine, or high grade) are made in this section they are taken directly from the manufacturer's catalog advertisements, and are not appraised values.

Bethlehem Furniture Company
Bethlehem, Pa.
bedroom suites

Bielecky Brothers
New York, N.Y.
summer furniture—willow ware

Blue Ridge Hickory Furniture
Company
High Point, N.C.
porch, lawn, cottage furniture

*Few people are familiar with
Tiffany Studios' furniture lines.
This is the inside back cover ad of a
1913* Arts and Decoration *magazine. Other Tiffany ads told potential customers of a selection of
colored sketches showing "sugges-
tions for the treatment of various
rooms," and that at the Studios
clients could see Tiffany's selection
of "antique and modern Furniture,"
as well as the more familiar Tiffany
Favril glass, leaded glass windows,
and lighting fixtures.*

Boston Mirror Company
Boston, Mass.
mirrors, frames, and molding

Boston Upholstering Company
Boston, Mass.
parlor furniture, couches, and
odd chairs

C. M. Bott Furniture Company,
Inc.
Buffalo, N.Y.
dining room furniture

Brown and Simonds Company
Somerville, Mass.
library tables, extension tables

Brown Furniture Company
Salisbury, N.C.
odd dressers, sideboards, chiffoniers, and buffets

C. G. Brown Furniture Company
Syracuse, N.Y.
china cabinets, bookcases, ladies'
desks, music cabinets, taborets

Butler Manufacturing Company
Syracuse, N.Y.
parlor cabinets, desks; tea, card,
nested, work, and parlor tables;
screens; hall clocks and chairs;
dining room, bedroom, and
library furniture

Capitol City Chair Company
Atlanta, Ga.
medium-grade chairs

Carlson, Bloomquist, and Snow
Jamestown, N.Y.
dining, parlor, library, and dressing tables, and sideboards

Carolina Furniture Company
Durham, N.C.
suites, dressers, beds, and stands

Carrollton Furniture
Manufacturing Company
Carrollton, Ky.
bedroom suites, bureaus, washstands, chiffoniers, dressing
tables, wardrobes

C. P. Caspersen
Titusville, Pa.
dining tables

Central Furniture Company
Rockford, Ill.
dining room furniture

Century Furniture Company
Grand Rapids, Mich.
dining room suites, living room
and library furniture

Charlotte Furniture Company
Charlotte, Mich.
bedroom furniture

Chicago Parlor Furniture
Company
Chicago, Ill.
parlor furniture

Cincinnati Chair Company
Cincinnati, Ohio
chairs, rockers, other furniture

Clinton Furniture Company
Lock Haven, Pa.
chamber suites

Colie and Son
Buffalo, N.Y.
upholstered furniture, couches,
parlor suites, odd pieces, Morris
chairs, and davenports

Collins-Hale Manufacturing
Company
Wilkes-Barre, Pa.
parlor suites, couches, Turkish and
easy chairs, rockers

Colonial Furniture Company
Boston, Mass.
Colonial furniture

Colonial Furniture Company
Newburgh, N.Y.
Colonial furniture

Colonial Manufacturing Company
Zeeland, Mich.
grandfather clocks

Conant Ball Company
Boston and Gardner, Mass.
chairs, tables, breakfast sets

Conewango Furniture Company
Warren, Pa.
odd and princess dressers,
chiffoniers, and robes

Continental Furniture Company
High Point, N.C.
bedroom furniture

Covert Furniture Company
Meridian, Miss.
chamber suites, bedsteads,
dressers

Coye Furniture Company
Stevens Point, Wis.
chamber suites, sideboards,
buffets, and chiffoniers

Crescent Furniture Company
Evansville, Ind.
sideboards, buffets, china closets,
chamber suites

Culler Furniture Company
Williamsport, Pa.
chamber furniture, chairs and
extension tables, chiffoniers,
cupboards, iron beds, sideboards,
stands

Davis-Birely Table Company
Shelbyville, Ind.
tables

Deiter, Jacob, and Sons Company
New York, N.Y.
parlor frames and furniture to
order

Detroit Cabinet Company
Detroit, Mich.
music cabinets, ladies' desks, secretaries; writing, sewing, parlor,
and tea tables; jardiniere stands

Diamond Furniture Company
Jamestown, N.Y.
parlor and library tables, taborets

Dixie Furniture Company
Lexington, N.C.
bedroom furniture

Doernbecher Manufacturing
Company
Portland, Oreg.
chamber suites, dressers, and
bureaus

C. A. Dorney
Allentown, Pa.
sideboards

Dubuque Cabinet Maker's
Association
Dubuque, Iowa
chairs, rockers, lounges; bedsteads, chamber suites, bureaus,
chiffoniers; hall racks; extension,
kitchen, and center tables; stands;
washstands; wardrobes; desks,
secretaries; Colonial furniture

Dunbar Furniture Manufacturing
Company
Berne, Ind.
upholstered furniture for living
rooms, hotels, and club rooms

Chas. E. Dunn
Buffalo, N.Y.
upholstered and antique furniture

Dunn and Salisbury
Keene, N.H.
high art dining, library, bedroom,
children's furniture, and fancy
chairs and rockers

Eagle Furniture Company Inc.
High Point, N.C.
chamber suites and dressers

Easton Furniture Manufacturing
Company
Easton, Md.
oak bedroom suites and sideboards

Eaton Chair Company
Chicago, Ill., and Monticello, Ind.
chairs

Elk Furniture Company
Lexington, N.C.
sideboards, chamber suites, odd
dressers, chiffoniers

O. R. Farr
Chesterfield, N.H.
tables

Findlay Table Mfg. Company
Findlay, Ohio
extension tables, pedestals, and
taborets

Forest City Furniture Company
Rockford, Ill.
libraries, combination cases, music
cabinets, ladies' desks, bookcases,
folding tables, washstands, beds

Forest Furniture Company
North Wilkesboro, N.C.
dressers, sideboards, and
washstands

Forsyth Furniture Lines
Winston-Salem, N.C.
bedroom and dining room
furniture, chairs

Fort Smith Furniture
Manufacturers' Company
(The Old Fort Lines)
Fort Smith, Ark.
conglomeration of companies
producing all types of furniture

Franchi-Forbes Furniture
Company
New York, N.Y.
Colonial and Dutch inlaid re
productions

Fremont Furniture Company
Fremont, Ohio
parlor and library tables and
taborets

French and Heald
Milford, N.H., and Boston, Mass.
chamber furniture, chiffoniers and
sideboards

William A. French Furniture
Company
Minneapolis, Minn.
cabinet-made furniture

L. Friedrich and Bro. Furniture
Company
St. Louis, Mo.
lounge frames, bookcases, desks,
parlor tables, and dressers

Henry Fuldner
New York, N.Y.
dining and side tables, sideboards,
china closets; special-order work

*Collectors are standing in line to bid
when fine-quality reproductions by a
highly respected and widely know
company like Margolis become
available at auction, no matter what
the location. The Margolis matching
late Sheraton/early Empire–style
bed (top) and dresser (above) were
sold at Neal Auction Company in
New Orleans, and the Chippendale-
style bow-front chest (opposite) at
Clearing House Auction Galleries in
Connecticut.*

Empire Furniture Company
Jamestown, N.Y.
chamber suites and odd dressers in
plain and quartered oak; cheap
and medium-priced goods

Emrich Furniture Company
Indianapolis, Ind.
sideboards, buffets, and tables

Max Englander
New York, N.Y.
upholstered furniture and bedding

Enterprise Furniture Company
Glen Rock, Pa.
chamber suites and sideboards

S. G. Estabrook and Company
New York, N.Y.
parlor and library furniture

Estey Manufacturing Company
Owosso, Mich.
bedroom furniture

Faribault Furniture Company
Faribault, Minn.
combination and library cases,
ladies' desks, buffets, and china
closets

L. G. Fullam and Sons
Ludlow, Vt.
porch, saddle-seat rockers, and
dining chairs

Gainesville Furniture
Manufacturing Company
Gainesville, Ga.
chamber suites, dressers, tables,
and chairs

Gate City Furniture
Manufacturing Company
Greensboro, N.C.
chamber suites, odd dressers,
chiffoniers

Gettysburg Manufacturing
Company
Gettysburg, Pa.
sideboards and hall racks

Globe Chair Company
Hillsboro, Ohio
cane and upholstered chairs

Globe Furniture Company
Evansville, Ind.
chamber suites

Globe-Home Furniture Company
High Point, N.C.
chamber suites, odd dressers, and
chiffoniers

R. W. P. Goff
Philadelphia, Pa.
china, music, and parlor cabinets;
side tables; pedestals; library
tables; hall stands; chairs

Goldstrom Bros.
Baltimore, Md.
parlor suites, couches, lounges,
Morris chairs, odd pieces

Grand Rapids Bookcase & Chair
Company
Hastings, Mich.
dining room furniture

Grand Rapids Chair Company
Grand Rapids, Mich.
chairs

Grand Rapids Fancy Furniture
Company
Grand Rapids, Mich.
ladies' desks, bookcases, music
cabinets, writing tables

Grand Rapids Furniture
Company
Grand Rapids, Mich.
dining room and living room
furniture

Grand Rapids Table Company
Grand Rapids, Mich.
parlor, den, library, and bedroom
tables

Gray and Company
New York, N.Y.
pier and mantel mirrors

Great Western Novelty Company
Zeeland, Mich.
commodes, china racks, dressing
stands

Greeman Bros. Manufacturing
Company
Batesville, Ind.
suites, sideboards, chiffoniers,
commodes

Greensboro Furniture
Manufacturing Company
Greensboro, N.C.
chamber suites, dressers,
chiffoniers

Gross and Hastings
Allegheny, Pa.
couches, lounges, davenports,
parlor suites, bedding

Hagerstown Table Works
Hagerstown, Md.
extension tables and stands

Hall and Lyon Furniture
Company
Waverly, N.Y.
bedsteads, dressing cases, princess
dressers, chiffoniers, ladies' dressing tables, and washstands in
quartered oak, bird's-eye maple,
and mahogany

Hanke Bros.
Chicago, Ill.
parlor desks, sideboards, china
closets, chiffoniers, bureaus,
washstands, odd dressers and
chamber suites

F. W. Hanpeter Furniture
Company
St. Louis, Mo.
bedrooom furniture

Harris Manufacturing Company
Springfield, Ohio
high-grade leather couches,
chairs, and davenports

Hastings Table Company
Hastings, Mich.
end tables, cabinets, writing tables

Hekman Furniture Company
Grand Rapids, Mich.
living room, library, hall furniture

F. Herhold and Sons
Chicago, Ill.
chairs, rockers, and settees

Hermann Furniture and Plumbers Cabinet Works
New York, N.Y.
bedroom suites; chiffoniers; odd dressers; bedroom and dining tables; wardrobes; bookcases; sideboards; hall stands, music cabinets; parlor, roll, flat-top, and standing desks

Herzog Art Furniture Company
Saginaw, Mich.
ladies' desks, music cabinets, center tables

Heywood Brothers and Wakefield Company
Baltimore, Md., and Gardner, Mass.
chairs, reed and rattan furniture

Hickory Furniture Company
Hickory, N.C.
suites and dressers

High Point Chair Company
High Point, N.C.
chairs and rockers

High Point Furniture Company
High Point, N.C.
chamber suites and odd dressers

Philip Hiss Company
Baltimore, Md.
interior woodwork, furniture, decorations, and special work to order

Hodell Furniture Company
Shelbyville, Ind.
mantel folding beds, dressers, chiffoniers, ladies' dressers, commodes

Holland Furniture Company
Holland, Mich.
bedroom furniture

Home Furniture Company Ltd.
York, Pa.
sideboards and dressers

Home Furniture Manufacturing Company
Pine Bluff, Ark.
chamber suites, chiffoniers

Hubbard, Eldredge & Miller (HEMCO)
Rochester, N.Y.
fancy chairs and rockers, living room and library chairs

Hughes Furniture Manufacturing Company
Baltimore, Md.
chamber suites, odd dressers, chiffoniers, wardrobes, hall racks, ladies' dressing tables, sideboards, and enameled dressers

B. F. Huntley Furniture Company
Winston-Salem, N.C.
all types

Illinois Parlor Furniture Company
Chicago, Ill.
upholstered furniture, couches, and odd pieces

Imperial Furniture Company
Grand Rapids, Mich.
gateleg tables, tables for all rooms, novelties

Indiana Furniture Company
Evansville, Ind.
bedsteads, chamber suites, extension tables, Victorian suites

Indiana Furniture Company
Connersville, Ind.
sideboards and buffets

Indianapolis Chair and Furniture Company
Indianapolis, Ind.
dining and office chairs, rockers, hall suites

Indianapolis Furniture Company
San Francisco, Calif.
furniture to order

Innis, Pearce and Company
Rushville, Ind.
chamber suites and chiffoniers

Jackson Glass Works
Jackson, Mich.
French and American mirrors, plates, and framed mirrors

Jacoby, Adam and Bro.
York, Pa.
sideboards in oak; dressers, chiffoniers, and washstands in plain and quartered oak, bird's-eye maple, mahogany, and curly birch

Jamestown Furniture Company
Jamestown, N.Y.
dressing tables, odd dressers, and
gentlemen's toilets

Janssen and Loeblein
Cleveland, Ohio
upholstered furniture, couches,
parlor suites, Morris chairs

T. H. Jenkins
Pittsburg, Kan.
parlor furniture, custom couches

DINING ROOM FURNITURE ONLY

A. J. Johnson and Sons Furniture
Company
Chicago, Ill.
china closets, buffets, sideboards,
plate racks, bookcases

Jason P. Johnson
Warren, Pa.
bedroom suites, chiffoniers

Johnson Chair Company
Chicago, Ill.
chairs

Johnson Furniture Company
Grand Rapids, Mich.
dining room and bedroom
furniture

C. E. Jorgenson
Chicago, Ill.
chamber suites, chiffoniers, bedsteads, bureaus, washstands, and
toilets in oak, elm, and maple

Peter Josten
Philadelphia, Pa.
breakfast, library, dining, kitchen,
center, extension, and pillar
extension tables

Kaal Rock Chair Company
Poughkeepsie, N.Y.
medium- and high-grade dining,
library, and office chairs in cane
and leather

Charles Kaiper's Sons
Cincinnati, Ohio
upholstered furniture

Karges Furniture Company
Evansville, Ind.
chamber suites, wardrobes,
dressers, and dressing tables

S. Karpen and Bros.
Chicago, Ill., and Michigan City,
N.Y.
bedroom chairs, upholstered
chairs, dining chairs

Keeler and Company
East Cambridge, Mass.
high-grade mahogany and oak
bed and dining room furniture

J. A. Kelley and Bros.
Clinton, Iowa
sofas, beds, davenports, reclining
chairs, couches, etc.

Theodore Kemnitz Furniture
Company
Green Bay, Wis.
chamber suites and odd dressers

Kenosha Crib Company
Kenosha, Wis.
parlor and library tables, jardiniere stands, taborets, cribs,
cradles, and beds

Kernersville Furniture
Manufacturing Company
Kernersville, N.C.
chamber suites, odd dressers,
commodes

Keystone Cabinet Company
High Point, N.C.
library furniture, davenports,
console tables

Kiel Furniture Company
Milwaukee, Wis.
tables

Kiel Manufacturing Company
Kiel, Wis.
dining, library, parlor, and kitchen
tables

Killian Brothers and Somma
New York, N.Y.
mahogany inlaid furniture

John Kimmeth and Company
Chicago, Ill.
upholstered furniture, parlor
suites, couches, odd chairs,
rockers, divans

Kincaid Furniture Company
Statesville, N.C.
bedroom suites and odd pieces,
chiffoniers, chevals

B. A. Kipp and Company
Milwaukee, Wis.
upholstered furniture

Joseph Kircher
Elkport, Iowa
special-order furniture

Kittinger Furniture Company
Buffalo, N.Y.
davenports, tables

H. W. Klemp
Leavenworth, Kan.
kitchen, dining room, and bedroom furniture, and extension
tables

E. J. Knapp Company
Chicago, Ill.
Colonial furniture

C. H. Knowles Furniture
Company
Fairfield, Maine
adjustable sofas, parlor suites, bed
lounges, couches, divans, chairs

K. P. L. Furniture Manufacturing
Company
Corry, Pa.
dressers, chiffoniers, washstands,
and combinations

Kroll Furniture Company
Allentown, Pa.
upholstered parlor furniture in
gold, gilt, and mahogany

Lane Company
Altavista, Va.
cedar chests

Laurens Furniture Manufacturing
Company
Laurens, S.C.

bedroom suites, chiffoniers, odd
dressers, and beds

Lawrenceville Manufacturing
Company
Lawrenceville, Va.
extension tables, sideboards, and
buffets

William Leavens and Company
Boston, Mass.
bookcases, cabinets, chairs,
Colonial and Mission furniture,
tables, and sideboards

Leroi Furniture Manufacturing
Company
St. Louis, Mo.
breakfast sets, chifforobes,
wardrobes, kitchen tables, and
bookcases

Level Furniture Company
Jamestown, N.Y.
bedroom furniture

Levin Bros.
Minneapolis, Minn.
couches, lounges, davenports,
parlor suites, and odd pieces,
upholstered furniture

Charles P. Limbert Company
Grand Rapids and Holland, Mich.
Holland-Dutch, Arts and Crafts
furniture

A. Lincoln and Son
Philadelphia, Pa.
bedroom furniture, bookcases,
chevals, wardrobes, nightstands,
and center tables

Little Rock Furniture
Manufacturing Company
Little Rock, Ark.

chamber suites, chairs, rockers,
and tables

Loomis and Hart Manufacturing
Company
Chattanooga, Tenn.
bedroom suites, wardrobes,
sideboards, dressers, washstands,
and tables

V. E. Lott and Company
Boston, Mass.
parlor and library furniture

Luce Furniture Company
Grand Rapids, Mich.
bedroom and dining room
furniture

Anthony Lucik
Cincinnati, Ohio
upholstered furniture, suites in
damask and leather; couches, davenports, ottomans, and odd pieces

Macey Company
Grand Rapids, Mich.
dustless-door bookcase

Thomas Madden Son and
Company
Indianapolis, Ind.
parlor suites, rockers, couches
and chairs, divans, davenports,
bed lounges

Maddox Table Company
Jamestown, N.Y.
parlor and library tables, taborets,
pedestals, Vernis-Martin tables,
and odd pieces

Maher Bros.
Medina, N.Y.
parlor suites, sofa beds, couches,
davenports, and odd pieces

J. F. Mahoney
Boston, Mass.
parlor furniture

Main Furniture Company
Hagerstown, Md.
sideboards, chamber suites, hall
racks, odd dressers, chiffoniers

Manchester Chair Company
Manchester, Ohio
dining chairs and rockers

Manistee Furniture Company
Manistee, Mich.
sideboards, buffets, and
chiffoniers

Mansfield Chair Company
Mansfield, Pa.
ladies' desks, bookcases, music
cabinets, hall racks

Marble & Shattuck Chair
Company
Cleveland, Ohio
dinner and office chairs

L. Marcotte and Company
New York, N.Y.
furniture to order

Marietta Chair Company
Marietta, Ohio
dining chairs and rockers, library
and bedroom chairs

Marshall Field & Company
(Home Crest Upholstered
Furniture)
Chicago, Ill., and New York, N.Y.
davenports, chaise lounges,
living room chairs

Wilson Marstellar
Philadelphia, Pa.

rockers; dining, cottage, office,
library, and upholstered chairs

Martin Furniture Company
Hickory, N.C.
sideboards and buffets

Maysville Manufacturing
Company
Maysville, Ga.
dining and kitchen chairs

J. H. McDanell's and Sons
Company
Warsaw, Ky.
chamber suites

Thomas H. McDonnell and
Company
Portland, Maine
upholstered furniture

McElroy and Nesbit Furniture
Company
Norcross, Ga.
beds, bureaus, kitchen safes,
tables, and suites

McKim and Cochran Furniture
Company
Madison, Ind.
dressers, stands, beds, chiffoniers,
wardrobes, toilets, suites

McLeod and Smith
Minneapolis, Minn.
upholstered furniture, parlor
suites, rockers, easy chairs, divans,
couches, davenports

Mechanics Furniture Company
Rockford, Ill.
sideboards, china closets, combination buffets, buffet, music, and
parlor cabinets in oak and
mahogany

Thomas W. Mellor
Philadelphia, Pa.
picture frames and parlor
furniture

Memphis Furniture
Manufacturing Company
Memphis, Tenn.
bedroom, living, dining, and
breakfast room furniture; odd
tables; chairs

George E. Messer and Company
Boston, Mass.
Old English designs of Colonial
furniture in mahogany

Michelson and Fischer
Rochester, N.Y.
dressers, chiffoniers, toilet tables,
beds, cheval glasses, ladies' desks,
washstands

Michigan Chair Company
Grand Rapids, Mich.
chairs

Miller Cabinet Company
Rochester, N.Y.
parlor and library tables, hall
seats, hanging glasses, hall racks,
pedestals, taborets, and stands

Milton Chair Factory
Milton, N.C.
chairs

Minneapolis Furniture Company
Minneapolis, Minn.
chamber suites, chiffoniers,
sideboards, folding beds

Mississippi Furniture
Manufacturing Company
Vicksburg, Miss.
general line of cheap and medium
goods

Mohlhenrich Furniture Company
Baltimore, Md.
bedroom and dining room
furniture

Lewis Morgan
Manchester, Mass.
chairs, sofas, desks, and bureaus

Morgan Manufacturing Company
Jamestown, N.Y.
parlor and library tables, taborets,
and pedestals

W. W. Motz
Lincolnton, N.C.
beds, bureaus, washstands, tables,
safes, desks, and furniture to order

Mt. Airy Furniture Company
Mt. Airy, N.C.
cheap and medium chamber
suites, odd beds, and dressers

Mt. Wolf Furniture Company
Mount Wolf, Pa.
sideboards, dressers, washstands

Mueller and Slack Company Inc.
Grand Rapids, Mich.
upholstered furniture

Linn Murray Furniture Company
Grand Rapids, Mich.
furniture, hall clocks, and chamber suites

Nashville Antique Furniture
Company
Nashville, Tenn.
antique furniture

National Chair Manufacturing
Company
Eldridge, N.Y.
chairs

National Furniture Company
Atlanta, Ga.
bedroom suites, sideboards,
buffets, hall racks, bookcases, and
combination cases

National Parlor Furniture
Company
Chicago, Ill.
upholstered furniture

New England Furniture Company
Grand Rapids, Mich.
sideboards, buffets, and closets

New England Reed Company
Boston, Mass.
chairs, reed and rattan furniture

New Orleans Furniture
Manufacturing Company
New Orleans, La.
chamber furniture and chairs,
kitchen safes, tables, and
wardrobes

Niemann and Weinhardt Table
Company
Chicago, Ill.
tables

J. R. Noell Manufacturing
Company
Danville, Va.
desks; extension, center, parlor,
saloon, and kitchen tables

A.C. Norquist Company
Jamestown, N.Y.
bedroom furniture

North-Western Cabinet Company
Burlington, Iowa
combination bookcases, ladies'
desks, and sectional cases

S. A. Nye Manufacturing
Company
Fairfield, Maine
desks, chiffoniers, folding tables,
bookcases, stands, center tables

Nypenn Furniture Company
Warren, Pa.
bedroom furniture

Oakland Manufacturing
Company
Winston-Salem, N.C.
bedroom suites, odd dressers,
chiffoniers, and sideboards

Oberbeck Bros. Manufacturing
Company
Grand Rapids, Wis.
sideboards, buffets, chiffoniers,
dressers, and chamber suites

J. G. O'Connell
Omaha, Neb.
parlor furniture

Ogden Furniture and Carpet
Company
Ogden, Utah
couches and parlor goods

Ohio Valley Furniture Company
Charleston, West Va.; Gallipolis,
Ohio; and Buffalo, N.Y.
oak chiffoniers, dressers, washstands, hall racks, sideboards,
buffets

Oklahoma Furniture Mfg.
Company
Oklahoma City, Okla.
general line of furniture

PALMER & EMBURY
MFG. CO.
WAREROOMS: 42-48 EAST 20TH ST.
OFFICES AND FACTORY: GOUVERNEUR SLIP
NEW YORK CITY

MANUFACTURERS OF THE
Highest Grades of PARLOR & LIBRARY FURNITURE
IMPORTERS OF COVERINGS FOR PARLOR SUITS, ETC,
A LARGE ASSORTMENT OF AUBUSSON, BELLEVILLE
AND NIMES TAPESTRIES IN STOCK

Olbrich and Golbeck
Chicago, Ill.
sideboards and buffets

Oscar Onken Company
Cincinnati, Ohio
hall clocks, cellarettes, ladies'
desks, sewing tables, pedestals,
taborets, cheval mirrors

Oregon Furniture Manufacturing
Company
Portland, Oreg.
bedroom and parlor suites,
dressers, kitchen furniture, flat-
top desks, chiffoniers, mattresses,
couches

Orinoco Furniture Company
Columbus, Ind.
parlor, library, dressing, and
writing tables; antique and
Colonial reproductions

Albert C. Otto
New York, N.Y.
reproductions of antiques, library
and hall furniture, café chairs and
tables

Ottowa Furniture Company
Holland, Mich.
sideboards, mahogany suites,
ladies' dressing tables, and
chiffoniers

Oxford Furniture Company
Oxford, N.C.
oak chamber suites, odd dressers,
and beds

Pacific Coast Lumber and
Furniture Company
San Francisco, Calif.
general line of furniture

C. S. Paine Company Ltd.
Grand Rapids, Mich.
mahogany upholstered furniture,
davenports, divans, chairs; odd
parlor, library, and hall pieces

Palmer and Embury
Manufacturing Company
New York, N.Y.
high-grade parlor and library
sofas, chairs, and tables;
taborets and pedestals; French
reproductions

Parkersburg Upholstering
Company
Parkersburg, W.Va.
parlor suites, couches, lounges,
chairs, and rockers

Parlor Furniture Manufacturing
Company
Cedar Rapids, Iowa
couches, parlor and library
furniture

J. E. Pearce and Company
New York, N.Y.
parlor suites; mahogany, gold
frame and stuffed suites; tapestry
and leather couches, frame and
Turkish armchairs and rockers,
divans, corner chairs, and window
and reception chairs in gold
frames

J. S. Peck and Son
Cardington, Ohio
dining and center tables

Penacook Furniture and
Upholstering Company
Concord, N.H.
parlor furniture

Penn Chair Company
Philadelphia, Pa.
cane- and wood-seat chairs and
rockers, rattan and porch chairs
and rockers

Penn Furniture Manufacturing
Company
Montgomery, Pa.
sideboards and buffets

Penn Upholstered Furniture
Company
Philadelphia, Pa.
parlor furniture and couches

Peters and Roberts Furniture
Company
Portland, Oreg.
parlor suites, chairs, lounges,
couches and mattresses

Phenix Furniture Company
Warren, Pa.
bedroom furniture

Philadelphia Furniture Company
Philadelphia, Pa.
parlor suites and couches

Phoenix Chair Company
Sheboygan, Wis.
dining room sets, breakfast sets,
Windsor chairs, high chairs, rockers, and lawn goods

Phoenix Furniture Company
Grand Rapids, Mich.
bed, dining, hall, den, and parlor
furniture

Phoenix Manufacturing Company
Covington, Ky.
library and parlor tables, music
cabinets, china cases, ladies' desks

Fred B. Pierce
Keene, N.H.
porch chairs

Pillon and Back
New York, N.Y.
special furniture to order

M. Pimes and Company
Baltimore, Md.
parlor suites, couches, lounges,
and upholstered goods

Pioneer Furniture Company
Eau Claire, Wis.
chamber suites, chiffoniers, and
sideboards

Plannett Manufacturing Company
Chicago, Ill.
picture frames and gilt furniture

Plymouth Furniture Company
Plymouth, Wis.
chamber suites, odd dressers,
chiffoniers and sideboards

Pooley Furniture Company
Philadelphia, Pa.
high-grade Louis, Empire,
Renaissance, Chippendale,
Sheraton, Adam, and Colonial
reproductions made to order after
original designs

Pottier and Stymus Company
New York, N.Y.
furniture to order

Pottsville Couch Company
Pottsville, Pa.
parlor furniture, couches, and
Morris chairs

R. Prescott and Son
Keeseville, N.Y.
chamber suites, dressers,
chiffoniers, washstands, and
bedsteads

Price Furniture Manufacturing
Company
Owensboro, Ky.
plain and quartered oak dining,
center, and library tables; hardwood dining and kitchen tables;
oak and hardwood bedsteads

Putnam Manufacturing Company
Baxter, Tenn.
bedroom suites, chiffoniers, sideboards, tables, odd dressers, and
washstands

John D. Raab Chair Company
Grand Rapids, Mich.
chairs

Randolph Furniture Works
Randolph, N.Y.
chiffoniers and dressers to match

Rann and Lenz
Chicago, Ill.
upholstered furniture

Readsboro Chair Manufacturing
Company
Readsboro, Vt.
folding chairs, lawn and porch
settees, folding card and lunch
tables

Red Wing Furniture Company
Red Wing, Minn.
chamber suites, dressers, combination cases, buffets, and beds

Reliable Furniture Manufacturing
Company
Baltimore, Md.
oak sideboards, chamber suites,
and dressers

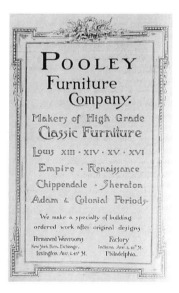

A. Renesch and Company
Cincinnati, Ohio
hall racks and settees, hanging
racks, cheval mirrors, dressing
tables

Rice-Carlston Furniture
Manufacturing Company
Minneapolis, Minn.
upholstered furniture

Richford Manufacturing
Company
Richford, Vt.
chamber furniture, odd bureaus,
chiffoniers, case work

J. E. Rilling and Company
Milwaukee, Wis.
upholstered furniture

J. K. Rishel Furniture Company
Williamsport, Pa.
chamber furniture and oak
extension tables

Rivers Furniture Company
Baltimore, Md.
oak chamber suites, chiffoniers,
sideboards and odd dressers

Riverside Furniture Company
St. Peter, Minn.
upholstered furniture

Frank A. Robart
Boston, Mass.
upholstered and antique furniture

Rockford Chair & Furniture
Company
Rockford, Ill.
dining and living room furniture

Rockford Palace Furniture
Company
Rockford, Ill.

buffets, china closets, sideboards,
music cabinets, ladies' desks, and
dressers

Rockford Republic Furniture
Company
Rockford, Ill.
dining room furniture

Rockford Standard Furniture
Company
Rockford, Ill.
china closets, library cases, buffets, and parlor desks

Colonial
Upholstered Furniture

ALSO TWO-PIECE SUITS OF
CHIPPENDALE, HEPPLEWHITE AND SHERATON

No. 742 Colonial Sofa

We manufacture our own Frames from
Special Designs

C. S. PAINE CO., LTD.

GRAND RAPIDS
MICH.

Henry Roesser and Son
Baltimore, Md.
chamber suites, sideboards, and
chiffoniers

Rome Furniture and Lumber
Company
Rome, Ga.
medium-grade suites, sideboards,
and chiffoniers in oak

Roos Manufacturing Company
Chicago, Ill.
cedar chests, easels, screens,
hat racks

Roper Furniture Company
Misawaka, Ind.
sideboards and buffets; pillar,
extension, dining, and library
tables; odd dressers, dressing
tables, chiffoniers in oak and
mahogany

C. F. Rowell and Bro.
Cedar Rapids, Iowa
parlor suites, odd pieces, couches,
davenports, and sofa beds

Royal Furniture Company
Grand Rapids, Mich.
bedroom, dining, and library furniture

Royal Parlor Furniture Company
New York, N.Y.
parlor suites and couches

St. Albans Furniture Company
St. Albans, Vt.
chiffoniers, bookcases, ladies'
desks, folding tables

St. Johns Table Company
St. John's, Mich.
extension, breakfast, kitchen, parlor, and library tables

Salamanca Furniture Works
Salamanca, N.Y.
chiffoniers and dressers

Salem Parlor Furniture Company
Winston-Salem, N.C.
upholstered furniture, lounges,
couches, and parlor suites

Salisbury Bros. Furniture
Company
Randolph, Vt.
oak, Mission, and Colonial
furniture

Anton Schaeffer
Covington, Ky.
parlor furniture

C. A. Schindler
West Hoboken, N.J.
antique furniture

E. J. Schneck and Sons
Allentown, Pa.
parlor and library tables and hall
stands

A. C. Schmidt and Company
Chicago, Ill.
upholstered furniture

Schock and Copelin
Manufacturing Company
Minneapolis, Minn.
parlor furniture frames, special
furniture, frames

Schulte Furniture Company
Cleveland, Ohio
parlor furniture, couches, odd
pieces, davenports, Turkish chairs,
and leather work

Seidel Furniture Manufacturing
Company
New Orleans, La.
cheap kitchen and bedroom
furniture

Selma Manufacturing Company
Selma, N.C.
general line of furniture

Seymour Furniture Company
Seymour, Ind.
bedroom suites and wardrobes

Sheetz-Straughn Manufacturing
Company
Indianapolis, Ind.
upholstered furniture

Shelbyville Wardrobe
Manufacturing Company
Shelbyville, Ind.
sideboards and buffets

J. Siehler
Baltimore, Md.
tables

Sikes Chair Company
Buffalo, N.Y.
cane and leather dining chairs
and rocking chairs

Simmons Furniture and Lumber
Company
Toccoa, Ga.
chamber suites and odd dressers
and beds

Elgin A. Simonds Furniture
Syracuse, N.Y.
chairs, tea wagons, ferneries,
aquarium tables, "quaint gifts"

M. Singer
New York, N.Y.
parlor suites, couches, and
odd pieces

Skandia Furniture Company
Rockford, Ill.
dining room suites

Skinner and Steenman
Grand Rapids, Mich.
sideboards and buffets

Sligh Furniture Company
Grand Rapids, Mich.
dressers, beds, writing tables,
nightstands

Ellis and Joyce Smith
Canastota, N.Y.
china closets, buffets, ladies' and
roll-top desks

George A. Smith
Boston, Mass.
general line of furniture

Somma Shops, Inc.
New York, N.Y.
tables, chairs, dining room suites

Casper Sommerlad
Brooklyn, N.Y.
antique and upholstered furniture

South Dunn Manufacturing
Company
Dunn, N.C.
chamber suites, odd dressers,
and chiffoniers

Southern Chair Company
High Point, N.C.
breakfast room suites

Southern Furniture Company
Atlanta, Ga.
sideboards, side tables, buffets,
chiffoniers, chamber suites,
dressers, and washstands

Southern Furniture Company
Texarkana, Tex.
suites, odd beds and dressers;
extension, kitchen, and parlor
tables; chiffoniers, sideboards,
bookcases, china closets, and
wardrobes

Specialty Furniture Company
Evansville, Ind.
bedroom furniture

Speiker Bros.
Zeeland, Mich.
Colonial clocks

Spencer and Barnes Company
Benton Harbor, Mich.
bedroom furniture, in mahogany,
walnut, bird's-eye maple, oak, and
figured red gum

George Spindler
Baltimore, Md.
parlor suites, couches, lounges,
bed lounges, Morris chairs,
Roman chairs, bedding

Lewis Spitz
New York, N.Y.
gold- and wood-frame mirrors

Ira M. Sprague Furniture Works
Keene, N.H.
tables

Springfield Furniture Company
Springfield, Ohio
bedroom suites, sideboards,
extension tables, kitchen safes,
beds and dressers

Standard Chair Company
Thomasville, N.C.
chairs and porch rockers

Standard Furniture Company
Lynn, Mass.
upholstered furniture

Star Furniture Company
Jamestown, N.Y.
odd dressers and commodes

Star-Hibriten Furniture Company
Lenoir, N.C.
bedroom furniture

Statesville Furniture Company
Statesville, N.C.
bedroom and dining room
furniture

John Stengel and Company
Dayton, Ohio
chamber suites, sideboards,
buffets, chiffoniers, and ladies'
dressing tables

Steul & Thuman Company
Buffalo, N.Y.
furniture suites

Stickley and Brandt Chair
Company
Binghamton, N.Y.
fancy and antique chairs, rockers
and settees, Morris chairs, and
Mission furniture

Stickley Brothers Company
Grand Rapids, Mich.
fancy chairs and tables

Stout and Wilson Furniture
Company
Salem, Ind.
sideboards, dressers, chiffoniers,
and commodes

H. M. Straussman and Company
Rochester, N.Y.
parlor and library suites, davenports, leather chairs, divans, fancy
chairs, and lodge furniture

Sudholt Lounge Company
St. Louis, Mo.
davenports, couches, odd pieces,
Morris chairs, parlor furniture,
and lounges

Comings Sweat Company
Richford, Vt.
chamber suites, dressers, chiffoniers

Tate Furniture Company
High Point, N.C.
chamber suites, odd dressers, and

chiffoniers in oak and imitation
mahogany

Tauber Parlor Furniture
Company
Chicago, Ill.
upholstered living room furniture

Taylor Chair Company
Bedford, Ohio
fine chairs and rockers

Tell City Furniture Company
Tell City, Ind.
chamber suites and wardrobes

Texarkana Table and Furniture
Company
Texarkana, Tex.
bedroom, dining, and kitchen
furniture

Thomasville Chair Company
Thomasville, N.C.
breakfast and dining room suites,
odd chairs

Thomasville Manufacturing
Company
Thomasville, N.C.
chiffoniers and dressers

H. J. Thompson Furniture
Company
New Duluth, Minn.
bedroom suites, chiffoniers, and
sideboards

Tipp Furniture Company
Tippecanoe City, Ohio
chamber suites, chiffoniers and
sideboards

Toledo Parlor Furniture Company
Toledo, Ohio
upholstered furniture

Toronto Furniture Company Ltd.
Toronto, Canada
bedroom and dining room suites

A. M. Tucker Furniture Company
Brookville, Ind.
chamber suites, chiffoniers, dressing tables, French dressers, and cheval glasses

Richard Tunk
Portland, Oreg.
upholstered furniture

Turkish Couch Bed Company
Boston, Mass.
couches

Udell-Predock Manufacturing Company
St. Louis, Mo.
parlor, library, and folding tables; pedestals and costumers

Union Furniture Company
Batesville, Ind.
chamber suites, chiffoniers and wardrobes to match in mahogany and oak

Union Furniture Company
High Point, N.C.
chamber suites, odd dressers, odd beds and washstands

Union Furniture Company
Rockford, Ill.
oak, walnut, birch, and mahogany furniture, combination cases, library cases, china closets, buffets, music and parlor cabinets

Union Furniture Company
Vevay, Ind.
bedroom suites, wardrobes, side boards, chiffoniers, and Victorian bedroom suites

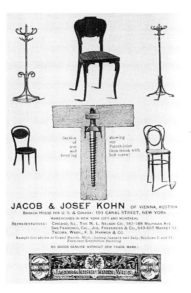

JACOB & JOSEF KOHN OF VIENNA, AUSTRIA
BRANCH HOUSE FOR U.S. & CANADA: 103 CANAL STREET, NEW YORK
WAREHOUSES IN NEW YORK CITY AND MONTREAL
REPRESENTATIVES: CHICAGO, ILL., THE M. L. NELSON CO., 187–188 MICHIGAN AVE.
SAN FRANCISCO, CALI., JOS. FREDERICKS & CO., 649–661 MARKET ST.
TACOMA, WASH., F. S. HARMON & CO.
Sample line shown at Grand Rapids, Mich., during January and July, Sections I. and II.
Furniture Exhibition Building
NO GOODS GENUINE WITHOUT OUR TRADE-MARK:
JACOB & JOSEF KOHN, WIEN

Union Specialty Works
Castorland, N.Y.
chairs and furniture specialties

United States Furniture Company
Evansville, Ind.
desks, secretaries, upright and mantel folding beds

Upham Manufacturing Company
Marshfield, Wis.
bedroom sets, sideboards, chiffoniers, buffets, French dressers

Urban, Daber, and Urban
New York, N.Y.
gilt furniture, three-piece suites, divans; reception, corner, and armchairs; tables and Roman chairs

Vaiden Lumber and Furniture Manufacturing Company
Vaiden, Miss.
hardwood and oak beds and suites

Valentine-Seaver Company
Chicago, Ill.
upholstered furniture, odd chairs, rockers, divans, ottomans, two- and three-piece suites, Colonial sofas, davenports, couches, and screens

Valley City Chair Company
Grand Rapids, Mich.
dining room, hall, and reception chairs, rockers, taborets, and parlor rockers

Vanstone Manufacturing Company
Providence, R.I.
special furniture to order

Van Vorst and Berman,
Los Angeles, Calif.
suites, chiffoniers, kitchen furniture, lounges, couches

Victor Chair Company
High Point, N.C.
cane- and split-seat cottage chairs, porch chairs, child's rockers and table chairs

Virginia Furniture Company
Martinsville, Va.
bedroom furniture

Virginia Table Company, Inc.
Marion, Va.
bedroom and dining room furniture

F. Vogel and Company
New York, N.Y.
parlor suites and odd pieces, dining room chairs, and china closets

Voit Bros.,
Brooklyn, N.Y.
parlor furniture and couches

Wabash Cabinet Company
Wabash, Ind.
special cabinet work to order

R. M. Wagan and Company
Mount Lebanon, N.Y.
Shaker chairs

Wagner Bros. Company
Canastota, N.Y.
couches and davenports

Wakefield Manufacturing
Company
Wakefield, Va.
bedroom suites

Wallweber Manufacturing
Company
San Francisco, Calif.
parlor furniture

Ward Furniture Manufacturing
Company
Fort Smith, Ark.
bedroom and dining room
furniture

Ware Manufacturing Company
Atlanta, Ga.
chamber suites, odd beds and
dressers, sideboards, wardrobes,
bookcases, kitchen safes, and
cupboards in oak and poplar

C. A. Warner and Company
New York, N.Y.
hall and shelf clocks, Mission and
Colonial designs

Warren Table Works
Warren, Pa.
Homer roll-top and extension
and dressing tables, dressers,
chiffoniers, commodes, and beds

Warsaw Furniture Mfg. Company
Warsaw, Ky.
hall furniture, combination bookcases, and library cases

Waterville Furniture Company
Waterville, Minn.
library cases, china closets, combination buffets, parlor desks, music
and parlor cabinets

Weber, Gottlieb and Company
Brooklyn, N.Y.
parlor furniture frames, dining
and odd chairs, and fancy couches

Webster Manufacturing Company
Minneapolis, Minn.
chairs

Weems-Lockwood Furniture
Company
Greenwood, Miss.
chamber suites, odd dressers,
beds, sideboards, wardrobes,
kitchen safes

M. J. Welter and Company
East Allentown, Pa.
parlor furniture, frames, and
odd pieces

W. Wengler and Son
Glasgow, Mo.
upholstered furniture

West Branch Novelty Company
Milton, Pa.
cedar chests, bamboo furniture,
taborets, and cheap ladies' desks

West Michigan Furniture
Company
Holland, Mich.
bedroom suites, sideboards,
buffets, chiffoniers, combination
commodes, odd dressers in elm,
oak, and mahogany

West York Furniture
Manufacturing Company
York, Pa.
ladies' desks, odd dressers, ladies'
toilet tables, and chiffoniers

Western Chair Company
Chicago, Ill.
wood, cane, and rattan chairs and
rockers

Western Furniture Company
Indianapolis, Ind.
chamber suites, chiffoniers, and
odd beds

Western Furniture and
Manufacturing Company
Wichita, Kan.
couches, lounges, davenports, and
parlor furniture; bedding, tables,
chamber suites

Western Parlor Frame Company
Chicago, Ill.
parlor furniture frames

Western Reserve Furniture
Company
Warren, Ohio
dressers, chiffoniers, and fine cabinet ware

Samuel L. Wheaton
Manchester, Mass.
hand-made furniture

Wheller-Okell Company
Nashville, Tenn.
four-poster beds

White Furniture Company
Mebane, N.C.
suites, dressers; center, library,
and extension tables

W. F. Whitney and Company
Ashburnham, Mass.
wood, cane, and reed chairs

Widdicomb Furniture Company
Grand Rapids, Mich.
bedroom furniture

J. C. Widman and Company
Detroit, Mich.
Colonial and Florentine mirrors,
parlor cabinets, hall furniture, and
chevals

Emil Wiener
Milwaukee, Wis.
upholstered parlor furniture,
couches, and library furniture

Williamsport Furniture Company
Williamsport, Pa.
chamber furniture, dressers,
chiffoniers, dressing tables, and
sideboards

Willingham Manufacturing
Company
Macon, Ga.
suites, odd dressers, beds, chairs,
rockers, center tables, sideboards

Winnebago Furniture
Manufacturing Company
Fond du Lac, Wis.
chamber suites, sideboards, chiffoniers, odd dressers, cheap beds

Wisconsin Furniture Company
Milwaukee, Wis.
extension, breakfast, kitchen,
library, office, and parlor tables

Wisconsin Manufacturing
Company
Jefferson, Wis.
wood-, cane-, and veneer-seat
dining chairs; floor and swing
rockers of wood, cane, veneer,
cobbler, or upholstered

I. H. Wisler and Sons
Philadelphia, Pa.
fine chairs

Wolverine Manufacturing
Company
Detroit, Mich.
parlor and library tables, taborets,
pedestals, jardinieres, and den
cabinets

Woodard Furniture Company
Owosso, Mich.
beds, dressers, washstands, chiffoniers, and ladies' dressing tables

T. G. Wooster Furniture
Manufacturing Company
Canaseraga, N.Y.
parlor furniture

Sometimes you have to snap a picture the best you can and live with the fact that if circumstances had only been better. I was in a small Florida town when a friend and I stopped by a house advertising a yard sale. There in the modest dining room was the only labeled Sypher piece I have ever seen! With much effort, we managed to get the corner cupboard far enough away from the wall so that I could get a picture of the label (opposite), but it was impossible with the camera and lens that I had with me to get a full shot of the tall, slender cupboard itself. I did the next best thing. I took a picture of the top section (left)—notice how it skims the ceiling—and then one of the bottom section (below). The cupboard itself is clearly a mixture of Chippendale-influenced motifs brought together at the late Victorian era. Remember, Sypher was the company so frequently referred to in Clarence Cook's The House Beautiful, *published in 1878.*

Wright and Lockhart
Boston, Mass.
chamber suites, bedsteads, bureaus, chiffoniers, washstands, somnoes, wardrobes, ladies' dressing tables, commodes, desks, cheval mirrors, chairs, rockers, tables

Wynne Furniture Manufacturing Company
Wynne, Ark.
general line of furniture

Yeager Furniture Company
Allentown, Pa.
parlor furniture, fancy and easy chairs, gold and gilt parlor pieces, weathered oak den furniture

Yorke Furniture Company
Concord, N.H.
suites, odd dressers, chiffoniers

Youngsville Manufacturing Company Ltd.
Youngsville, Pa.
chamber suites and sideboards

Ypsilanti Reed Furniture Company
Ypsilanti, Mich.
reed chairs and rockers, porch and lawn goods

Zanesville Mantel and Furniture Company
Zanesville, Ohio
sideboards, dressers, washstands, and chiffoniers

Zangerle & Peterson Company
Chicago, Ill.
parlor furniture frames and upholstered furniture

THE MAGICAL NAMES

When collectors and others seriously interested in American-made reproduction furniture discuss the very finest makers, those whose works are representative of the best in design, craftsmanship, and quality, some names come up over and over. Wallace Nutting, of course, is always included for his name is the best known. Then there is Margolis in Hartford, Connecticut; Potthast of Baltimore; Charack, Paine, and Beacon Hill in Boston; Valentine and Biggs in Richmond, Virginia; W. K. Cowan and David Zork in Chicago; Erskine-Danforth, Sypher, and Tiffany and Company in New York, which, believe it or not, made reproduction furniture at the turn of the century. Invariably someone mentions a few of the many other such companies that are regionally known. In my part of the world I immediately think of the Newcomb Company in Durham, North Carolina, and Mr. Howardton in tiny Clarksville, Virginia. But these are not nationally known companies as the others are. Unfortunately, none of the larger companies and practically none of the smaller shops are still around. They have, however, been replaced by other fine craft shops that are listed in the directory. But if you come upon a piece marked Margolis or Nutting or any of the others, this is a guarantee of fine-quality furniture.

Zeeland Furniture Manufacturing Company
Zeeland, Mich.
bedroom suites, hotel dressers, toilet commodes, sideboards, chiffoniers, and odd dressers

E. and O. Zucchi and Company
New York, N.Y.
Colonial furniture

THE AMERICAN CABINET MAKER,

Currently Working Craftsmen

Though most readers of this book will enjoy searching for the older pieces of American-made reproduction furniture, others who are interested in commissioning that special piece, an heirloom for tomorrow, will find this listing of craftsmen and craft shops making custom reproduction furniture helpful. Note that some craftsmen have catalogs available for a small fee, whereas others will send a brochure with the receipt of a self-addressed, stamped, business-size envelope.

Gary S. Adriance
288 Gulf Road
South Dartmouth, MA 02748
Catalog available.

Tom Bainbridge
R.D. 1, Box 207A
Oley, PA 19547
Catalog available.

John Bernstein
5900 Green Spring Avenue
Baltimore, MD 21209
SASE for brochure.

Christopher Bretschneider
Box 12
Shoreham, VT 05770
Catalog available. Makers of fine reproductions who use traditional joinery and hand-rubbed finishes. Send $5 for photos.

Teri Browning
P.O. Box 131
Wentworth, NH 03282

Period reproductions made with traditional techniques and finishes. Send $3 for a brochure.

Matthew Burak
P.O. Box 279
Danville, VT 05828
Custom eighteenth- and nineteenth-century furniture. Send $5 for catalog.

Cornucopia, Inc.
P.O. Box 1
Harvard, MA 01451-0001
SASE for brochure.

Lawrence Crouse
P.O. Box 606
Kearneysville, WV 25430
Catalog available.

Curin & Tarule
Box 3031
Plymouth, MA 02361
Furniture reproductions and woodwork from the seventeenth

century, handmade using period tools and methods. Send $2 for a brochure.

Peter J. DiScala
43 VanSant Road
New Hope, PA 18938
Handmade, hand-painted pine reproduction furniture with crackled finish. Send $2 for a catalog.

Donald A. Dunlap
15 Goodell Road
R.R. 2, Box 39
Antrim, NH 03440
Antique reproductions with hand-rubbed finishes and hand-cut joinery. Send $2 for a brochure.

Craig Farrow
P.O. Box 534
Watertown, CT 06795
Write for more information on fine seventeenth- and eighteenth-century reproductions made "the old way" with old tools.

Robert Ian Gale-Sinex
100 South Baldwin Street
#406
Madison, WI 53703
SASE for brochure. Eighteenth- and nineteenth-century veneered and inlaid reproductions.

Jeffrey P. Greene
1 West Main Street
Wickford, RI 02852
Eighteenth-century techniques and tools used to individually handcraft reproductions. Send $5 for a catalog.

D. T. Gutzwiller & Son
777 Mason Morrow Road
Lebanon, OH 45036

Traditionally joined and finished reproductions of eighteenth- and nineteenth-century pieces. Send $5 for a catalog.

Chris Harter
P.O. Box 125
Madison, NY 13402
Traditional construction techniques and hand finishing used to reproduce eighteenth-century furniture. Send $3 for a brochure.

Headley & Hamilton
Route 1, Box 1245
Berryville, VA 22611
Send for a free flyer picturing the handmade reproductions of eighteenth-century furniture.

Kenneth Heiser
195 East Yellow Breeches Road
Carlisle, PA 17013
SASE for brochure.

Michael Houle
P.O. Box 1089
Marstons Mills, MA 02648
Catalog available.

Howe & Braskie
237 Old Tilton Road
Canterbury, NH 03224
Traditional Shaker chairs and tables are handcrafted. Custom orders filled. Send a SASE for brochure.

Louis Irion III
1 South Bridge Street
Christiana, PA 17509
SASE for brochure. Eighteenth-century reproductions are traditionally crafted.

(Photo courtesy Leonard's)

David Le Fort
293 Winter Street
Hanover, MA 02339
Fine handcrafted and hand-carved American eighteenth-century reproductions are signed and dated. Brochure and catalog available.

Leonard's
600 Taunton Avenue
Seekonk, MA 02771
Catalog available. Period beds reproduced by hand.

Log House Sales Room
Berea College Crafts
Berea, KY 40404
SASE for brochure.

Roger Z. Mason
P.O. Box 438
Williamsburg, VA 23187
Furniture is handcrafted, and custom orders are filled. Send $2.75 and SASE for brochure.

Paul S. Miller
P.O. Box 703
East Berlin, PA 17316
SASE for brochure.

Moser Furniture Company
409 Fifth Street
Lynchburg, VA 24502

Brendan Murphy
2757 Lydius Street West
Schenectady, NY 12306
Catalog available.

Alan W. Pease
R.R. 1, Box 65
Richardson Road
Ashby, MA 01431
Custom reproductions of beds
and eighteenth- and nineteenth-
century period furniture are made
by hand. Send $4 for catalog.

William A. Pease
17 Fresh Meadow Drive
Lancaster PA 17603
High-style and country furniture
reproductions, case clocks, and
custom orders done using hand
tools and period techniques.
Send SASE for brochure or $5
for catalog.

Jim Rantala
8909 Toad Lake Road
Elisworth, MI 49729
SASE for brochure. Period techniques are employed in the making
of Windsor chairs and other
pieces.

Walter Raynes
4900 Wetheredsville Road
Baltimore, MD 21207
SASE for brochure. Eighteenth-
and nineteenth-century reproduc

tions are bench-made to order with
traditional tools and materials.

C. W. Riggs
P.O. Box 158
St. Mary's, WV 26170
Period tools and methods are used
in the making of Windsor chairs
and country furniture. Send $3 for
brochure.

Bryce M. Ritter
100 Milford Road
Downingtown, PA 19335
Antique wood and materials
are used in the construction of
eighteenth- and nineteenth-
century reproductions. Pieces are
finished with aged milk paint.
Send $3 for photos.

Glenn Sawyer, Jr.
5321 Cleveland Street, #202
Virginia Beach, VA 23462
Handmade reproductions are
made with distressed wood and
finished with crackled milk paint.
Send $2 for catalog.

Roger W. Scheffer
Straw Hill, Route 1
West Unity, NH 03743
Traditional methods used to
construct Windsor chairs.
Send $2 for catalog.

Thomas Schwenke
390 Main Street
Ridgefield, CT 06877
Federal furniture reproductions
taken from original designs and
using the same materials and
construction techniques. Send
$15 for catalog.

Woody Scoville
R.R. 1, Box 65
East Bank Road
East Calais, VT 05650
Windsor chairs of the eighteenth
century traditionally made, with
milk paint or stain and oil finish.
Send $1 for brochure.

Suter's of Virginia
2610 South Main Street
Harrisonburg, VA 22801 or
4200 West Broad Street
Richmond, VA 23230
Handcrafted Colonial reproduction
furniture made in walnut,
mahogany, and cherry. SASE for
brochure or $8.50 for a full catalog.

John Sullivan
50 Allen Street
Braintree, MA 02184
SASE for brochure. Hand-fitted
and -joined custom-made period
reproductions.

Ted Sypher
69 Richards Road
Chenango Forks, NY 13746
SASE for brochure. Fine furniture
reproduced using period tools and
construction techniques.

William Tillman
R.D. 3, Box 93
Stewartstown, PA 17363
SASE for brochure. Exact copies
of period pieces made using
vintage methods and materials.

Gergory Vasileff
740 North Street
Greenwich, CT 06831
Seventeenth- and eighteenth-
century reproductions are handcrafted, signed, and dated. Send
$5 for brochure.

William E. Wallick
41 North 7th Street
Wrightsville, PA 17368
Windsor chairs (including children's), settees, and tables are made in the traditional manner and finished with distressed paint. Send $2 for brochure.

Eldred Wheeler
60 Sharp Street
Hingham, MA 02043
Long-established and well-known for excellent quality reproductions.

Robert Wilkins
480 Guthrie Court
Winston-Salem, NC 27101
Wilkins' reproduction furniture is included in the Blair House collection.

Wright Table Company
P.O. Box 518
Morganton, NC 28680
Brochure and catalog available.

Museums, Libraries, and Exhibits

The Bernice Bienenstock
Furniture Library
1009 North Main Street
High Point, NC 27262
910-883-4011

Furniture Discovery Center
101 West Green Drive
High Point, NC 27260
919-887-3876

Grand Rapids Public Library
60 Library Plaza, NE
Grand Rapids, MI 49503
616-456-3600

The Little White House
Georgia Department of Natural Resources
Georgia Highway 85 West
Warm Springs, GA 31830
706-655-5870

McFaddin-Ward House
1906 McFaddin Avenue
Beaumont, TX 77701
409-832-1906

Maymont
1700 Hampton Street
Richmond, VA 23220
804-358-7166

Wallace Nutting Collection
Berea College
Berea, KY 40404
606-986-9341

Public Museum of Grand Rapids
272 Pearl Street
Grand Rapids, MI 49503
616-456-3977

Reynolda House Museum of American Art
Reynolda Road
Winston-Salem, NC 27116
910-725-5325

Rhode Island School of Design
Museum of Art
224 Benefit Street
Providence, RI 02903
401-454-6507

Roosevelt-Vanderbilt National Historic Sites
249 Albany Post Road
Hyde Park, NY 12538
914-229-9115

Stan Hwyet Hall
714 North Portage Path
Akron, OH 44303
216-836-5535

Swan House
Atlanta History Center
130 West Paces Ferry Road, NW
Atlanta, GA 30305-1366
404-814-4000

Van Steenberg Library
Kendall College of Art and Design
111 North Division Avenue
Grand Rapids, MI 49503
616-451-2787

Voigt House
115 College Avenue, SE
Grand Rapids, MI 49503
616-456-4600

Whitehall, The Flagler Museum
Coconut Row
Palm Beach, FL 33480
407-655-2833

Winterthur Library
The Henry Francis duPont
Winterthur Museum
Wilmington, DE 19735
302-888-4600

Pricing
Guidelines

While it is good to know the style and approximate age of a piece of furniture, there is a lot more to know as well. What is it worth? is a question I am asked constantly.

As an appraiser, I am the first to stress the importance of knowing the value of your belongings. You only have to drop by a furniture store or glance at a newspaper or magazine advertisement to realize how expensive new reproduction furniture is these days. But the cost of new reproduction furniture can be quite different from the prices of old reproduction furniture.

New furniture is priced according to the manufacturer's labor and material costs combined with the retail store's overhead, plus such variables as shipping and advertising. Though prices for identical pieces of furniture can vary according to where the furniture is being sold and if it is on sale, the price spread has established parameters. Manufacturers' suggested retail prices can be considered a guideline to pricing.

On the other hand, the value of true antique and period furniture is established in the sec-

ondary market—antiques shops, auctions, estate sales, and so forth. In those arenas, the price for each piece of furniture is determined by its quality, rarity, age, condition, and the public's demand for comparable or similar pieces.

For example, most simple, circa 1840, one-drawer cherry wood tables, of which untold numbers were made, can be expected to be priced somewhere in the range of $250 to $500. The quality of the wood, the lines and proportion of the table, and its condition will determine where it falls on that scale.

But a rarer, circa 1780, Hepplewhite inlaid mahogany Pembroke table can be expected to be priced higher. The simpler of these tables will usually sell for anywhere between $2,000 and $4,000. And the Hepplewhite-period Pembroke table with exceptional inlay and shaped drop leaves, rather than the straight drop leaves, will sell for closer to $10,000.

At present, old reproduction furniture is floundering in the marketplace. When, for example, a circa 1917, good-quality, mass-manufactured Hepplewhite sideboard is offered in the arena where most period pieces are being sold, no one may be interested in what is perceived as a "second-best" piece. The reproduction Hepplewhite-style sideboard may be almost "given away" for $500 or $600.

But what happens when the same sideboard is marketed to potential buyers who are accustomed to the 1990s' manufactured sideboards made of wood parts and flimsily constructed? Now the old reproduction sideboard is praised for being more than seventy-five years old, make of mahogany, and having good, solid construction. Under these optimum conditions that "giveaway" sideboard may be quickly snatched up for $2,500.

For this reason, combined with the vast differences in the quality of mass-manufactured reproduction furniture (see chapter 7), it is virtually impossible to establish accurate, reliable prices. However, there are general guidelines you can follow when assessing the value of old reproduction furniture—when purchasing it or selling it. That is what I have provided for you here—pricing *guidelines* which, when used in combination with the reminders mentioned next, plus knowing where to look and what to look for when scrutinizing a piece of furniture for quality, will be your first step to assessing the value of a particular piece.

Remember to Stop, Look, and Think

- Quality is the single most important factor in determining value.
- Never overlook the design; good lines and proportions are fundamental to the value of a piece of furniture.
- Look for good, solid construction elements that will wear well in the years to come.
  - Cheap materials are used sometimes and can be disguised, so check carefully. Buckling, warping, and splitting are all telltale signs of poor construction and inexpensive materials.
  - Alterations can devalue old reproductions the same way they do antiques.
  - Intricate decorative motifs (carving, inlay) require additional time and expert craftsmanship to execute even in mass-produced furniture. This goes the same for such parts as legs, spindles, stretchers, bedposts, and stiles.
- Faithful reproductions are considered more desirable than those pieces that combine several different style elements.
- Furniture made by well-known companies and craftsmen are particularly desirable and will hold their value.

A CORNER IN THE GALLERIES OF EMIL FEFFERCORN

The BEAUTY
of the ANTIQUE

Admiration for the beauty of fine antique furniture is not merely an affectation.

It is a recognition of the intrinsic beauties of old forms, old colors, old romance.

The works of the master-designers of the past have never been excelled, and the best furniture of today is the antique or the worthy reproduction.

The Galleries of Emil Feffercorn contain a collection of *unusual antiques of absolute authenticity.* The shops of Emil Feffercorn also produce *perfect reproductions.*

Mr. Feffercorn extends a cordial invitation to visit the galleries and will be pleased to make appointments with out of town clients.

EMIL FEFFERCORN
126 and 128 East 24th Street
NEW YORK CITY

PRICING GUIDELINES FOR THE MOST COMMONLY FOUND PIECES OF REPRODUCTION FURNITURE

GOOD QUALITY (but often the design may be weak or not true to the original style)
FINE (well-constructed, quality materials, good design)
EXCEPTIONAL (with attributes such as hand-rubbed finish or hand-carved motifs, custom-made or by a well-known designer)

JACOBEAN STYLE	GOOD QUALITY	FINE	EXCEPTIONAL
Side chairs	$75–$150	$200–$325	$500–$800
Armchairs	$100–$350	$325–$600	$650–$2,500*
Sofas/settees	$150–$350	$200–$500	$250–$1,500**
China presses, cabinets	$450–$750	$600–$1,200	$1,500–$3,500
Chests, highboys	$200–$500	$450–$1,000	$850–$1,500
Desks, ladies'	$350–$700	$500–$1,000	$750–$2,000
Desks, large	$350–$800	$750–$1,500	$1,200–$2,800
Dining tables	$500–$800	$750–$1,800	$1,200–$2,500
Occasional tables	$75–$250	$150–$325	$300–$650
(also small benches, plant stands, music, cabinets, etc.)			
Secretary-bookcases	$250–$800	$500–$1,800	$900–$2,500
Sideboards/serving tables	$250–$750	$500–$1,500	$1,200–$3,200
Beds, low posts	$95–$250	$175–$350	$325–$600
Beds, tester	$150–$500	$500–$1,500	$750–$3,000

* Many fine- and excellent-quality Jacobean-style armchairs were upholstered in rich, sometimes antique, tapestry. The presence of such fashionable upholstery can strongly affect the value of such chairs.

** Traditionally upholstered pieces have a much lower resale potential than wooden case pieces (chests, tables, cupboards, and so on). If using this table as a guideline for insurance, rather than selling or buying pieces, the cost of expensive upholstery should be figured in on top of the suggested values given in the table above.

QUEEN ANNE STYLE	GOOD QUALITY	FINE	EXCEPTIONAL
Side chairs	$95–$225	$250–$395	$500–$1,000
Armchairs	$100–$400	$375–$725	$650–$1,500
Wing chairs	$75–$250	$125–$350	$250–$1,500
Sofas/settees	$150–$350	$200–$500	$250–$2,500
Cabinets, cupboards	$450–$750	$600–$1,200	$1,500–$2,800
Chests	$200–$500	$500–$1,200	$850–$1,500
Desks, ladies'	$350–$700	$500–$1,000	$750–$2,000
Desks, large	$350–$800	$500–$1,500	$1,200–$2,800
Highboys	$595–$895	$850–$1,600	$1,200–$7,500
Dining tables	$500–$800	$750–$1,800	$1,200–$2,500
Occasional tables	$75–$250	$150–$500	$500–$1,200
(also small benches, plant stands, music cabinets, etc.)			

	GOOD QUALITY	FINE	EXCEPTIONAL
Secretary-bookcases	$450–$895	$750–$2,200	$1,200–$5,000
Sideboards, serving tables, lowboys	$250–$950	$500–$1,800	$1,200–$3,500
Beds, low posts	$95–$250	$175–$450	$425–$800
Beds, tester	$250–$500	$500–$1,600	$850–$3,000

CHIPPENDALE STYLE*	GOOD QUALITY	FINE	EXCEPTIONAL
Side chairs	$95–$225	$250–$500	$500–$1,200
Armchairs	$100–$400	$375–$825	$650–$1,500
Wing chairs	$75–$250	$125–$350	$250–$1,500
Sofas/settees	$150–$350	$200–$500	$250–$3,200
Cabinets, cupboards	$450–$750	$600–$1,500	$1,500–$3,500
Chests	$200–$500	$500–$1,200	$850–$1,800
Desks, ladies'	$350–$700	$500–$1,000	$750–$2,000
Desks, large	$350–$800	$500–$1,500	$1,200–$4,200
Highboys	$595–$895	$850–$2,500	$1,200–$7,500
Dining tables	$500–$800	$750–$1,800	$1,200–$2,800
Occasional tables (also small benches, plant stands, music cabinets, etc.)	$75–$250	$150–$500	$500–$1,500
Secretary-bookcases	$450–$895	$750–$2,200	$1,200–$5,000
Sideboards/serving tables, lowboys	$250–$950	$500–$1,800	$1,200–$3,500
Beds, low posts	$95–$250	$175–$450	$425–$800
Beds, tester	$250–$500	$500–$1,600	$850–$3,000

* When fretwork that turns a Chippendale-style piece into a Chinese Chippendale–style piece is present, you can expect to pay more for the fancier-looking piece.

ADAM AND FEDERAL STYLES (Hepplewhite and Sheraton)	GOOD QUALITY	FINE	EXCEPTIONAL
Side chairs	$75–$150	$200–$325	$500–$800
Armchairs	$100–$350	$325–$600	$650–$1,500
Martha Washington chairs	$75–$250	$125–$450	$250–$1,200
Sofas/settees	$150–$350	$200–$500	$250–$1,500
China presses, cabinets	$450–$750	$600–$1,200	$1,500–$3,500
Chests	$200–$500	$450–$1,000	$850–$1,500
Desks, ladies'	$350–$700	$500–$1,000	$750–$2,000
Dining tables	$500–$800	$750–$1,800	$1,200–$2,500
Occasional tables (also small benches, plant stands, music cabinets, etc.)	$75–$250	$150–$325	$300–$650
Secretary-bookcases	$250–$800	$500–$1,800	$900–$2,500

	Good Quality	Fine	Exceptional
Sideboards, serving tables	$250–$750	$500–$1,500	$1,200–$3,200
Beds, low posts	$95–$250	$175–$350	$325–$600
Beds, tester	$150–$500	$500–$1,500	$750–$3,000

EMPIRE AND VICTORIAN*	GOOD QUALITY	FINE	EXCEPTIONAL
Side chairs	$50–$125	$95–$225	$300–$500
Armchairs	$75–$150	$100–$300	$225–$850
Sofas/settees	$125–$350	$150–$500	$225–$1,200
China presses, cupboards	$250–$450	$350–$750	$800–$1,500
Chests	$150–$500	$350–$650	$500–$850
Desks, ladies'	$250–$500	$400–$650	$500–$1,000
Desks, large	$350–$800	$500–$1,200	$1,000–$2,200
Dining tables	$500–$800	$750–$1,800	$1,200–$2,500
Occasional tables	$45–$150	$100–$225	$225–$500
(also small benches, plant stands, music cabinets, etc.)			
Secretary-bookcases	$250–$500	$350–$1,200	$750–$2,200
Sideboards, serving tables	$150–$500	$300–$1,200	$500–$1,800
Beds, low posts	$65–$150	$95–$250	$225–$450

* Because period pieces from these two styles still abound, there is less demand for Empire and Victorian reproductions. However, period pieces are often larger-scaled than reproductions. Further, many reproductions are in better condition than the older period pieces. At present, however, reproductions of these two styles are less appealing to the public and have a limited market.

LOUIS XV AND XVI*	GOOD QUALITY	FINE	EXCEPTIONAL
Side chairs	$75–$150	$200–$325	$500–$1,000
Armchairs	$100–$350	$325–$750	$650–$2,500
Sofas/settees	$150–$350	$350–$800	$500–$3,200
Cabinets	$450–$750	$750–$1,600	$1,500–$4,500
Chests	$200–$500	$450–$1,500	$950–$3,500
Desks, ladies'	$350–$800	$500–$1,750	$850–$3,200
Desks, large	$350–$1,000	$550–$2,200	$1,200–$3,800
Dining tables	$500–$800	$750–$1,800	$1,200–$2,500
Occasional tables	$75–$250	$150–$500	$450–$1,750
(also small benches, plant stands, music cabinets, etc.)			
Secretary-bookcases	$250–$800	$500–$2,200	$1,200–$4,500
Sideboards, serving tables	$250–$750	$500–$1,800	$1,200–$4,200

* Really superior quality French-style reproduction furniture is in great demand. The cost of the materials (exotic woods, bronze mounts), combined with the craftsmanship required to make these pieces, made these pieces expensive when they were first created. Demand plus quality equals high value.

Bibliography

American Collector. New York: Collectors Publishing Co., 1930s and 1940s.

American Manufactured Furniture. West Chester, Pa.: Schiffer Publishing Ltd., 1988.

Andrews, John. *The Price Guide to Victorian, Edwardian and 1920s Furniture (1860–1930).* Woodbridge, Suffolk, UK: Antique Collectors' Club, 1980.

Arts & Decoration. New York: Adam Budge, 1910–19.

Axelrod, Alan, ed. *The Colonial Revival in America.* New York: W. W. Norton, 1985.

Baker Guide to Good Furniture: Being a treatise on the making, selection, use and care of furniture with special emphasis on the subject of Eighteenth Century Reproductions. . . . Holland, Mich.: Baker Furniture Company, 1947.

Boger, Louise Ade. *Furniture Past & Present.* New York: Doubleday & Company, 1966.

Bok, Edward W. *Twice Thirty: Some Short and Simple Annals of the Road.* New York: Charles Scribner's Sons, 1925.

Burchell, Sam. *A History of Furniture—Celebrating Baker Furniture: One Hundred Years of Fine Reproductions.* New York: Harry N. Abrams, 1991.

Butler, Joseph T. *American Antiques 1800–1900: A Collector's History and Guide.* New York: The Odyssey Press, 1965.

Callahan, John C. *The Fine Hardwood Veneer Industry in the United States: 1838–1990.* Lake Ann, Mich.: National Woodlands Publishing Co., 1990.

Campbell, Nina, and Caroline Seebohm. *Elsie de Wolfe: A Decorative Life.* New York: Panache Press, 1992.

Clifford, C. R. *Period Furnishings, Third Edition, 1922.* New York: Clifford & Lawton.

Columbian Gallery: A Portfolio of Photographs of the World's Fair. Chicago: The Werner Company, 1894.

Cook, Clarence: *The House Beautiful: Essays on Beds and Tables, Stools and Candlesticks.* New York: Scribner, Armstrong and Company, 1878.

Daniels, Fred Hamilton. *The Furnishing of a Modest Home.* Worcester, Mass.: The Davis Press, 1908.

Darling, Sharon. *Chicago Furniture: Art, Craft & Industry, 1833–1983.* New York: W. W. Norton & Company, 1984.

Dean, Ben H., and Walter J. Peterson. *Modern American Period Furniture: A Guide to the Selection of Harmonious Furnishings for the American Home of Today.* Grand Rapids, Mich.: Periodical Publishing Company, 1917.

Dewing, Maria Richards. *Beauty in the Household.* New York: Harper & Brothers, 1882.

Dietz, Ulysses G. *Century of Revivals: Nineteenth-Century American Furniture from the Collection of the Newark Museum.* Newark, N.J.: Newark Museum of Art, 1983.

Dyer, Walter A. *The Lure of the Antique.* New York: The Century Company, 1910.

Eastlake, Charles L. *Hints on Household Taste in Furniture, Upholstery and Other Detail.* 1868 (republished many times since).

Eberlein, Harold Donaldson, and Abbot McClure. *The Practical Book of Period Furniture.* Philadelphia: J. B. Lippincott Company, 1914.

Eberlein, Harold Donaldson, et al. *The Practical Book*

of Period Furniture: A New Edition with Supplement on Modern Decoration. Philadelphia: J. B. Lippincott Company, 1931.

Fairbanks, L., and Elizabeth B. Bates. American Furniture: 1620–Present. New York: Richard Marek Publishers, 1981.

Federhen, Deborah A., et al. Accumulation & Display: Mass Marketing Household Goods in America, 1880–1920. Winterthur, Del.: The Henry Francis du Pont Winterthur Museum, 1986.

Fitzgerald, Oscar P., guest curator. The Green Family of Cabinetmakers: An Alexandria Institution, 1817–1887. Alexandria, Va.: The Alexandria Association, 1986.

Freeman, John. Wallace Nutting Checklist of Early American Reproduction. Watkins Glen, N.Y.: American Life Foundation & Study Institute, 1969.

Furniture: As Interpreted by the Century Furniture Company. Grand Rapids, Mich., 1937.

Furniture: Its Selection and Use. Washington, D.C.: U.S. Government Printing Office, 1931.

Furniture Dealers' Reference Book. Chicago, 1926 and 1927.

Furniture Manufacturer's Reference Catalog. Chicago: American Homes Bureau, 1927–1928.

Furniture World and Furniture World South. New York: 1870 to the present.

Giedion, Siegfried. Mechanization Takes Command. New York: W. W. Norton and Co. by arrangement with Oxford University Press, 1969.

Good Furniture: The Magazine of Good Taste. Grand Rapids: The Dean-Hicks Company, 1910–1932.

Grand Rapids Furniture Record, The. 1900–1939, microfilm available from Norman Ross Publishing Inc., 330 West 58th Street, New York, N.Y. 10019.

Herts, Benjamin Russell. The Decoration and Furnishing of Apartments. New York: J. P. Putnam's Sons, 1915.

Holloway, Edward Stratton. The Practical Book of Furnishing the Small House and Apartment. Philadelphia: J. B. Lippincott, 1922.

Home, 1923, The. Chicago: Woman's Weekly.

Homefurnishing Arts. Chicago, 1934.

House Beautiful Furnishing Annual, The. Boston: The Atlantic Monthly Company, 1926.

International Studio. New York, 1910s–1930s.

Israel, Fred L. 1897 Sears Roebuck Catalogue. New York: Chelsea House Publisher, 1968.

Ivankovich, Michael. The Guide to Wallace Nutting Furniture. Doylestown, Pa.: Diamond Press, 1990.

Kaempffert, Waldemar, ed. A Popular History of American Invention. New York: Charles Scribner's Sons, 1924.

Kebabian, Paul B., and William C. Lipke, eds. Tools and Technologies: America's Wooden Age. Burlington: University of Vermont, 1979.

Kranzberg, Melvin, ed. Technology in Western Civilization. Volume I. New York: Oxford University Press, 1967.

Lamb, George N. The Mahogany Book. Chicago: Mahogany Association, n.d.

Lewis, Arnold, et al. The Opulent Interiors of the Gilded Age. New York: Dover Publication, Inc., 1987.

Lindquist, David P., and Caroline C. Warren. Colonial Revival Furniture. Radnor, Pa.: Wallace-Homestead Book Company, 1993.

Lockwood, Luke Vincent. Colonial Furniture in America. New York: Charles Scribner's Sons, 1901.

Lydens, Z. Z., ed. The Story of Grand Rapids. Grand Rapids, Mich.: Kregle Publications, 1966.

Lynes, Russell. The Tastemakers. New York: Harper & Brothers, 1955.

Lyon, Irving Whitall. Colonial Furniture of New England. Boston and New York: Houghton Mifflin Company, 1891.

Magazine Antiques, The. New York: 1922 to the present.

Mayhew, Edgar de N., and Minor Myers, Jr. A Documentary History of American Interiors: From the Colonial Era to 1915. New York: Charles Scribner's Sons, 1980.

Monkhouse, Christopher P., and Thomas S. Michie. American Furniture in Pendleton House. Providence: Museum of Art, Rhode Island School of Design, 1986.

Morningstar, Connie. Flapper Furniture and Interiors of the 1920s. Des Moines, Iowa: Wallace-Homestead Book Company, 1971.

Morse, Frances Clary. Furniture of the Olden Time, New Edition. New York: The Macmillan Company, 1936.

Naeve, Milo M. *Identifying American Furniture: A Pictorial Guide to Styles and Terms, Colonial to Contemporary.* Nashville, Tenn.: The American Association for State and Local History, 1981.

Nutting, Wallace. *Wallace Nutting General Catalog. Supreme Edition.* 1930. Reprint, Atglen, Pa.: Schiffer Limited, 1978.

————. *Wallace Nutting's Biography.* Framingham, Mass.: Old America Company Publishers, 1936.

Oliver, J. L. *The Development and Structure of the Furniture Industry.* London: Pergamon Press, 1966.

Parsons, Frank Alvah. *Interior Decoration: Its Principles and Practice.* Garden City, N.Y.: Doubleday, Page & Company, 1916.

Pattou, Albert Brace, and Clarence Lee Vaughn. *Furniture: Furniture Finishing, Decoration and Patching.* Wilmette, Ill.: Frederick J. Drake & Co., 1955.

Payne, Christopher, *The Price Guide to 19th-Century European Furniture.* Woodbridge, Suffolk, UK: Antique Collectors' Club, 1981.

Post, Emily. *The Personality of a House: The Blue Book of Home Design and Decoration.* New York: Funk & Wagnalls Company, 1930.

Quimby, Ian M. G., ed. *Material Culture and the Study of American Life.* New York: W. W. Norton & Company, A Winterthur Book, 1978.

Quimby, Ian M. G., and Polly Anne Earl, eds. *Winterthur Conference Report 1973: Technological Innovation and the Decorative Arts.* Charlottesville: University Press of Virginia, 1973.

Randel, William Pierce. *The Evolution of American Taste.* New York, Crown Publishers, 1978.

Ransom, Frank Edward. *The City Built on Wood: A History of the Furniture Industry in Grand Rapids, Michigan, 1850–1950.* Ann Arbor, Mich.: Edwards Bros., 1955.

Rhoads, William B. *The Colonial Revival.* New York: Garland Publishing, 1977.

Seal, Ethel Davis. *The House of Simplicity.* New York: The Century Company, 1926.

Seale, William. *The Tasteful Interlude: American Interiors Through the Camera's Eye, 1860–1917.* New York: Dover Publications, 1990.

Sell, Maud Ann, and Henry Blackman Sell. *Good Taste in Home Furnishing.* New York: John Lane Company, 1915.

Shackleton, Robert, and Elizabeth Shackleton. *Adventures in Home-Making.* Philadelphia: Curtis Publishing Company, 1909.

————. *The Quest of the Colonial.* New York: The Century Company, 1907.

Smith, Jane S. *Elsie de Wolfe: A Life in the High Style.* New York: Atheneum, 1982.

Smith, Ray C. *Interior Design in 20th-Century America: A History.* New York: Harper & Row Publishers, 1987.

Stillinger, Elizabeth. *The Antiquers.* New York: Alfred A. Knopf, 1980.

Story of a Developing Furniture Style: Fiftieth Anniversary Edition, The. Fayetteville, N.Y.: L & L. G. Stickley Inc., 1950.

Sutcliffe, G. Lister, ed. *Legacy of Wood and Woodworking.* Harrisburg, Pa.: National Historical Society, 1990.

Swedberg, Robert W., and Harriett Swedberg. *Furniture of the Depression Era.* Paducah, Ky.: Collector Books, 1987.

Sypher & Company. *The Housekeeper's Quest: Where to Find Pretty Things.* New York: 1885.

Throop, Lucy Abbot. *Furnishing the Home of Good Taste.* New York: McBridge, Nast & Co., 1910.

Vollmer, William A., ed. *A Book of Distinctive Interiors.* New York: McBride, Nast & Company, 1912.

Wallick, Ekin. *Inexpensive Furniture in Good Taste.* New York: Hearst's International Library, 1915.

Weidman, Gregory R. *Furniture in Maryland, 1740–1940.* Baltimore: Maryland Historical Society, 1984.

White, Trumbull, and William Igleheart. *The World's Columbian Exposition, Chicago, 1893.* Philadelphia: International Publishing Company, 1893.

Whiton, Sherrill. *Elements of Interior Decoration.* Chicago: J. P. Lippincott Company, 1932.

Williams, Henry Lionel, and Ottalie K. Williams. *How to Furnish Old American Houses.* New York: Bonanza Books, 1969.

Wilson, Richard Guy, et al. *The Machine Age in America, 1918–1941.* New York: The Brooklyn Museum, in association with Harry N. Abrams, Inc., 1986.

Winterthur Portfolio. Chicago: University of Chicago Press, 1965.

Wright, Richardson. *House & Garden's Second Book of Interiors.* New York: Condé Nast Publication, Inc., 1920.

Furniture Company Catalogs and Pamphlets Consulted for This Text

AUTHOR'S NOTE: Over the years I have both purchased old furniture company catalogs when I could find them in used- and rare-book stores and pored through the ones preserved in public and private museums and libraries. These once plentiful, now scarce, records of the furniture companies are harder and harder to find. The following list of a random sampling of these catalogs is arranged by company and cites the type of furniture illustrated in each. Often these catalogs are not dated, and in some cases, the covers and first pages are missing, so it's only possible to guess at the date. Though only a smattering of the catalogs used in the research and writing of this book are included here, this list may be beneficial to readers looking for information on specific companies.

Albert Grosfeld, Inc. New York, New York. Catalogs from the 1930s and 1940s of European-inspired reproductions.

Aulsbrook and Jones Furniture Company. Sturgis, Michigan. Catalog from the 1920s of reproduction furniture based on traditional styles.

Baker Furniture Factories. Allegan, Michigan. The 1932 catalog of reproductions based on seventeenth- and eighteenth-century English, American, and French styles; 1933 supplement; 1950s catalogs.

Beacon Hill Collection. Boston, Massachusetts. W. & J. Sloan's catalog of the famed Beacon Hill reproduction line.

Berkey & Gay Furniture Co. Grand Rapids, Michigan. A 1920s portfolio of various reproduction lines for the different rooms in the house based on classical styles.

Biggs. Richmond, Virginia. A 1930s catalog of "antiques for future generations" based on American eighteenth- and nineteenth-century styles.

Caro-Craft. Sharpsburg, North Carolina. Various catalogs of eighteenth-century American styles.

Carrollton Furniture Manufacturing Company. Carrollton, Kentucky. A 1916 catalog of reproductions loosely based on classical styles.

Charak Furniture Company. Boston, Massachusetts. A 1940s catalog showing a wide variety of classically nspired reproduction furniture copied from English and American antiques.

Chittenden & Eastman Company. Burlington, Iowa. A 1922 catalog of the company's Square Brand line.

Devon Shops, Inc. New York, New York. A 1938 catalog of decorative furniture.

Early American Built by Stickley of Fayetteville. Fayetteville, New York. A 1930s catalog of rooms based on period designs.

Elmer O. Stennes' Early American Clocks and Parts. Weymouth, Massachusetts. Catalog of grandfather, grandmother, and banjo clocks.

Imperial's Jeffersonian Group. Grand Rapids, Michigan. Genuine "old-fashioned," solid-mahogany furniture.

J. D. Bassett Mfg. Company. Bassett, Virginia. A 1940 catalog of bedroom, dining room, and dinette furniture showing the use of "exotic" veneers and the "waterfall" furniture so popular at the time.

Johnson Furniture Company. Grand Rapids, Michigan. A 1938 catalog showing adapations of period styles.

Kittinger Manufacturing Company. Buffalo, New York. A 1928 catalog of fine-quality reproductions based on period English furniture.

Kroehler Book of Living Room Arrangements. Naperville, Illinois. A 1920s catalog showing room arrangements based on reproduction furniture styles.

Lewis Mittman Inc. New York, New York. A 1960s catalog of "Three Centuries of Reproductions."

Moser Furniture Company. Lynchburg, Virginia. Handmade reproductions ranging from Chippendale-style secretaries to Victorian upholstered parlor pieces (see page 81 and 83).

Murphy DoorBed Company. New York, New York. The 1924 yearbook.

National Chair Manufacturing Corporation. Asheboro, North Carolina. Mid-1930s catalog of houshold furnishings including "thrifty" lines.

Shearman Brothers Company. Jamestown, New York. Upholstered funiture based on classical styles, 1931–1932.

Suter's Handcrafted Furniture. Harrisonburg, Virginia. Case and upholstered furniture based on eighteenth- and early nineteenth-century American furniture forms (see page 82).

Tell City Chair Company. Tell City, Indiana. Tell City primer of early American home decorating.

Todhunter. New York. Late 1920s catalog showing "authentic reproductions" of Colonial mantels.

Virginia Craftsmen Inc. Harrisonburg, Virginia. A 1930s catalog "Being the latest showing of Authentic Reproductions and Adaptations of Early American Furniture."

Richard Wheelwright. New York, New York. Adaptations of European styles.

Williamsburg Restoration Reproductions. Williamsburg, Virginia. Catalogs featuring reproductions based on the mostly English Colonial Williamsburg collection.

Wood & Hogan. New York, New York. Distinguished English reproductions.

Acknowledgments

This book has been in my mind for ten-plus years. Over that time everyone who has known of my fascination with the subject, and who is also interested in reproduction furniture, has sent me clippings, old ads, even books and catalogs related to the subject. I cannot thank you enough. Nor can I sufficiently thank all the used- and rare-book dealers who have put aside materials they thought I would be interested in.

These people, especially, have spent their valuable time assisting me in compiling the information and illustrations: Carl Vuncannon, Melva Teague, and Karla Webb at The Furniture Library; Shelby Labbon at the Furniture Discovery Center; Michael Ivankovich; Eddy Portnoy at Norman Ross Publishers; Dick Harms, archivist at the Grand Rapids Public Library; Jeannie Larson, Bryan Kwapel, and Chris Carron at the Public Museum of Grand Rapids; Chris Ham at Voigt House; Neville Thompson at the Winterthur Library, Henry Francis du Pont Museum; Charles Sutton; Richard Barentine, director of the Furniture Factories Marketing Association of the South in High Point, North Carolina; Nancy K. Lester and Frances Westbrook at the Atlanta History Center; Dan Farrell of the Antique Collectors' Club; Stephen Dennis; Margaret Tramontine at Stan Hwyet Hall; Rosemarie George, who introduced me to the treasures at Stan Hwyet; Sterling Boyd; Nick Bragg at Reynolda House Museum of American Art; Garry Barker at Berea College; Jessica Foy and Matt White at the McFaddin-Ward House; Robert W. Skinner, Inc.; Robert S. Brunk; Clearing House Auction Galleries; Sam Pennington; Charles and David Moser of Moser Furniture; Carol Suter Michael at Suter's of Virginia; Alex Mitchell at Baker Furniture Company; Robert Colleen at Kindel; Anne Jordan at Eleanor Roosevelt National Historic Site; John and Linda Neal, Neal Alford, Maggie Cantwell, Lauri Clay, David Nicolay, and Ruth Winston at Neal Auction Company; Betty Baker; Victoria Buresch; Liz Seymour; and especially Annique Dunning. Thank you, Annique, for your untiring efforts.

Thank you also to my many and very special friends at Crown Publishers, especially my editor, Sharon Squibb, who continue to carry on Crown's long-established tradition of bringing information on antiques and collectibles to the reading public.

And a special note of appreciation to my children, Langdon and Joslin, who for years have patiently waited while I poked through old-book stores and took "just one more picture" when I had promised them I wouldn't. Just remember, by the time you're my age, these reproductions will be your antiques.

Index